4½ Networking Mistakes

Maximize your Networking Efforts by Avoiding Common Mistakes

By Tiffanie Kellog

Acknowledgments

There are so many people I wish to acknowledge, and I am sure I will miss a few. I love you all!

Thanks to my husband, Rob, who supports me, almost unconditionally, in everything I do!

Thanks to Tom Fleming, who helped put me on the path of referral marketing via the Referral Institute®, and with the spectacular life I live today.

Thanks to my brother Robert for his help with marketing and in making the book more interesting.

Thanks to a few people who helped by sharing their wisdom by being a contributing author (amongst other assistance): Courtney Nestler, Dawn Lyons, Dr. Ivan Misner, Paula Bonnell, Phil Bedford, and Tom Fleming.

Thanks to the people who helped make this book happen, the beta readers, people who pre-purchased the book, and offered advice on the content and cover. Including, and not limited to: Tonya Lonsbury, Russ Critendon, Jason Avery, Enrico Saltarelli, Tim McClain, Patti Lustig, Laura Ellingham, Kathryn Lang Sever, Nancy Ellen Hale, Tonya Acha, Margo Currey, Charles Kitzmiller, Shawn Yesner, Terri Scarcelli, Darlene Sheets, Melissa Rodgers, Gary Myers, Phillip Pasek, Bob & Pam Janoske, Matt Wilkerson, Cami Miller, Ben Pugliesi, Murrie Ives, Lizzette Sarria, Claudia Lowry, Kristian Grønli, Gary Williams, Jay Doty, Susan Sands, Kelly Santos, Christopher Clarke, Larry Gastley, Paula O'Neil, Ph.D., Chris, Stacey & Z Janoske, Jamie Blake, Ginny Cannon, Caroline Roe, Shirley Pheasant, Paula Delage, Randy Keirn, Carolyn Quintin, Louise Walsh, Catherine Price, Ken Donaldson, Michael Anthony, Grace Barfield, Jill Kinney, Janet Stephens, Pamela Sprecher, Jennifer Gentile, Michael Carli, Gailen Spinka, Dave Johnson, Robert Burmaster, Jacquiline Skelton, David E. Albaugh, Lisa Langan, Chris Krimitsos, Jackie Wood, Gail Nott, and Karen Barrese.

Thanks to everyone for your help!

Table of Contents

Forward

There are a TON of books out there about networking. And here you are, reading another one.

What makes this book different?

I am going to teach you to do the opposite of what you are told to do by so many other networking books tell you to do. Why?

In the coming pages, I hope to share with you a better way to network.
Please note, I am not necessarily saying their advice is wrong, I am saying there is an alternative (and better) way to network.

Throughout the book, I am going to explore with you, in what I hope to be a humorous way, the things to avoid when networking, followed by tips on how to be a masterful networker. In the final chapters you will find additional information, including a more detailed look at how to do what is explored at the book's beginning.

For those of you who choose never to read the how-to part, that is okay. In the first part of the book you will learn enough of the dos and don'ts of networking to become a powerful networker.

As a professional speaker, trainer and facilitator, I have had the pleasure over the past decade of sharing this material via the Certified Networker® Program from the Referral Institute®, mainly in the Tampa Bay area. As I am unable to reach the entire world from Tampa Bay, I wanted to create what I thought would be the best book on networking.

In addition to what I have learned through speaking on referral marketing, I have asked several colleagues, friends and even my husband to contribute to Networking Nuggets and Bonus Materials. Again, special thanks go to Tom Fleming, who taught me about funneling conversations and coined the phrase, "Book a Meeting, from a Meeting."

I hope you enjoy reading, and as always, happy networking.

The Problem with Networking

What is networking?

A misunderstanding of what networking is often is where most problems begin.

When asked why they network, entrepreneurs most often say they network to get more business. And it is this mindset that brings people to networking events: "I *network* so I can get new prospects to buy from me."

The problem with this line of thinking is the people who attend networking events rarely come with the intent of "buying something today." They attend the events ready to sell, and I would say they are actually **prospecting** rather than **networking**. This misunderstanding helps explain why so many people think networking just does not work. When you go into an event wanting to sell, and no one is there to buy, of course you are going to say "It does not work."

The true purpose of networking, in my opinion (which you care at least a little about or you would not be reading this book), is to meet people to add to your network of referral sources.

Will there be some people at these events who may become clients of yours? Of course! Know, though, there is another group of people at networking events who can be **even more valuable** to you than clients. I am getting ahead of myself.

When networking, your goal should be to **book a meeting** from the initial meeting as there often are dozens, or even hundreds, of people in the room and it is impossible to meet them all. The important point is identifying the right people and scheduling a meeting to learn more about your common business and personal interests, so you can begin to develop relationships beneficial to both parties.

Over the next several chapters, we are going to explore the *4½ Networking Mistakes* that even the experts tell you to make. We will explore:

- How to avoid in-person spamming.

- Why your name tag is probably hurting more than helping you when networking.

- Why networking alone will not help you grow your business.

- What is an effective system to utilize when networking.

- How to develop stronger relationships.

- How the 19 Networking Nuggets in Section Two can help you achieve amazing results when networking.

As you go through the book, know I have made each and every mistake that I write about. Experts tell us to do this or that, and you want to do what the experts encourage you to do. I did too!

It was not until I discovered the Referral Institute® that I realized the various things I had been doing could have been done better. This book is here to help you avoid the same mistakes.

Throughout the chapters, you will encounter **eTiffanie**s.

You may wonder what an **eTiffanie** is. Originally, I planned to call these **Tiffanie's Tips**, as they are crucial points to pull from each section.

A few years ago, William Mellas, a financial advisor and client of mine, coined the phrase **eTiffanie**. Think of an epiphany: a sudden, intuitive perception of, or insight into, the essential meaning of an event or circumstance, usually initiated by some simple, commonplace experience. Then, instead of epiphany, insert TIFFANIE, and what you are left with is an **eTiffanie** — an epiphany from Tiffanie!

In the third section, some issues are revisited in the form of Bonus Material. The Bonus Material goes in-depth on a few topics that add value to what already has been discussed in the book.

Hold on and enjoy the ride!

P.S.: You may be intrigued by the "½ mistake," which might be a reason you bought the book. How could there be half a mistake?

The mistakes explored in the book are things that many networking experts tell you to do, while the half mistake is one that only a few experts tell you to do. Hence, the half a mistake — and a touch of creative marketing from me.

4½ Networking Mistakes

Mistake #1: In-Person Spamming

Simon walks into the networking event. He has been in business for less than a year and is worried because the business is struggling. Simon has found the Internet to be a wealth of knowledge and sees networking as a way to grow his business. That is why he is here.

He carries a stack of business cards in his pocket, ready to pass them out to each person he meets, as recommended by many experts. Simon makes his way through the crowd, handing a business card to each person. Some people smile, take his card and continue with their conversation, while others eye his card with interest before moving on to the next person.

At the end of the event, Simon walks out excited. He has passed out almost 100 cards. He gets into the office early the next morning, anticipating the calls and emails that will be flooding his way. But the day passes slowly, and today turns into tomorrow, and into the next week.

Simon is at a loss as to why no one he handed a card to has contacted him. Depressed, he determines networking does not work for him and goes back to cold calling.

Where did Simon go wrong?

The experts share: "Pass out business cards to people you meet." If you have been to even one networking event, you may have had someone you just met hand you a business card, even though you did not ask for it. It may have felt as if you were assaulted or the victim of a "hit-and-run," where the card was thrust into your hand as the person said, "I have to run, but I wanted you to have my card." In many of these situations you were not even asked for your card in return.

You were a victim of in-person spamming!

We are familiar with spam that comes via our email (or texts, Facebook messages, etc.) and people know it is wrong to send spam. When people give you their business card without being asked, it is often ineffective and most are unaware of their offense.

In examining why people in-person spam, besides the fact that experts told them to do it, here are a few rationalizations they may have:

- "Everybody really needs my product/service. While I don't have time to talk to everyone, I want them to have my card so they can do business with me."

- "My card is so amazing that people will see it, call me, and do business with me. I don't even need to talk to them."

- "I just met you, and you don't know me, here's my card, so call me maybe?" (Apologies to Carly Rae Jepsen!)

None of those scenarios are likely to result in business.

Let's take a look at in-person spamming done another way:

A gentleman, Ted, walks into a bar. Ted is looking for "the woman of his dreams"; however, he has only 20 minutes to make the connection and the bar is packed with patrons. Ted came prepared. He has little pieces of paper with his name, phone number and "I'm looking for love, call me" written on it. Armed with his slips of paper, he proceeds to walk up to every person, male and female, in the bar and passes on his information.

You might be thinking, every person? Men and women! Why both?

Ted gave the papers to the all the women because he is hoping one might be *"the* woman." The men? Ted wanted them to pass his information along in case they know a lovely woman who also is looking for love.

Because of his time constraints, after he passes out his slips of paper, Ted leaves. He has another bar to visit so he can meet even more people.

Ted, in his quest for love, is doing what so many people do while business networking, in-person spamming. It is no wonder why this method is ineffective. Networking is very much like Ted's search for true love, except when networking, instead of looking for love we are looking for business relationships. Networking is the opportunity to "interview" people briefly to see if you want to add them to your network.

While we are on the subject of "dating," take a look at speed dating. In speed dating, there is a boy's side and a girl's side, with each sitting across from the other. Each prospective couple is allowed a few minutes to get to know the other before a bell is rung and one side slides down one seat to talk to the next person. At the end of the event, each person hands the facilitator a sheet of paper identifying the people he or she liked. The facilitator compares the notes and if both people in the pairing indicated they would like to know each other better then the information is exchanged. If only one person — or neither — is interested, then there is no need to exchange information. Why would you want to continue a conversation with someone if you do not see the potential for the relationship to move forward?

Applying this to networking, the exchange of the business card should happen only if both parties are looking to continue the conversation beyond the event.

How will you know that the other person is interested? You will be asked for your business card.

eTIFFANIE: When networking, give your business card ONLY when you are asked!

With the request of your card you now have permission and you are delivering what has been requested of you; you are no longer guilty of in-person spamming. What if you are not asked for your business card and you believe there is potential for a business relationship moving forward? While you could simply wait for people to ask you for your card or be disappointed at the end of the conversation when they did not, there is another option.

There is a technique called mirroring that can work in this situation. If you want them to have your business card, then ask the person "May I please have one of your business cards?" Hopefully, once you have a card, you will be asked for yours, too. That is your permission to finally give your card to the person with whom you are speaking. If you are not asked for your card, then comes the hard part: DO NOT offer your card. The person you have been speaking with is telling you they are uninterested in continuing the conversation beyond the event.

There could be many reasons why people do not ask for your card:

- They already have a strong relationship with someone who does what you do.

- They also do what you do.

- For some reason, they may not like you. You have seven seconds to make a first impression and sometimes we rub people the wrong way when we first meet them, which could be because of our behavioral style.
  (See *Bonus Material on Behavioral Styles*).

- They do not believe in the product/service you offer.

- They are having a bad day, or do not like your shoes, or any other unknown reason.

Regardless of the reason, by not asking you for a card, you do not have permission to offer it.

Think about being at a bar, and there is that guy who keeps talking to an uninterested woman, and all the girl can think is, "How do I get rid of this guy?" Don't be that annoying guy (or girl).

Combat Networking Mistake #1: In-Person Spamming, by remembering:

eTIFFANIE: When networking, give out your business card ONLY when you are asked!

Author's Note:

What happens if you are a victim of in-person spamming when networking?

When networking, I use two different pockets or different places in my purse, to hold cards after I receive them. One pocket is for people with whom I would like to follow up. The other pocket is a holding spot for people who have in-person spammed me. If you are making notes on the back of cards, you also could simply write 'IPS' for in-person spammer.

Networking Mistake #1 ½: "Here is a card for you and one to pass on"

"It's so nice to meet you, Betty," said Angie, as she reached for her business cards. "I want to make sure you have my business card. Here is one for you, and one you can pass on to someone who needs my product."

Betty slid the cards into her pocket then moved on to speak to the next person at the event.

Some experts encourage people, when networking, to pass out multiple business cards when making a new acquaintance. The reason for this tip is the expectation that a first meeting will create additional referrals. Hence, you ensure the person has extra cards to pass along at will.

Unfortunately, Angie's meeting with Betty is simply the beginning of the relationship and there is a low likelihood of Angie being referred.

Will there ever be a time when you meet a person who knows someone else in dire need of your product/service? Yes! This does happen, occasionally; it is a rare occurrence instead of the norm.

Most often when someone like Angie passes out multiple business cards while networking, those cards end up in the trash. Why? Because people you have just met are rarely in a position to refer you. Why not? Because there is not yet **trust** between the two of you!

A common saying is people do business with those they **"know, like, and trust."** This same process holds true with referrals. Unless there is an immediate need, people refer only those they already "know, like, and trust." On that lucky occasion where there is a pressing need for your product or service, most often the person you are talking with will tell you so and request another card on the spot or use the card already in hand to forward your information.

As our culture shifts, so does the importance of business cards. In the past, perhaps even up to a decade ago, it was important to have multiple cards to pass along. Business cards were rarely discarded, as they were the single place with all your contact information. You even wanted the extra cards.

Nowadays, when you give someone a business card, what happens to it?

- The **master networker** takes your card, completes any necessary follow-up actions, adds the contact to a database, and then usually throws it away. (A master networker may even file the card.)

- The **average networker** might go back to the office and add the information to a database.

- The **beginner networker** collects cards that unfortunately end up in a stack, or drawer, bowl, etc., with all the other business cards collected, often gathering dust.

- The **annoying networker** adds your email address to the distribution list of email blasts sent out regularly — an irritating and illegal practice that should never be done!

In the electronic age of CRM (customer relationship management software), databases, and smartphones, most people store their contact information electronically. In addition, Google and online databases (Google+, Facebook, LinkedIn, Twitter, etc.) can be searched for information on particular people, and connect with them almost instantly.

eTIFFANIE: Connect ONLINE with people you meet in person to begin building the "know, like" of "know, like, and trust."

The ½ networking mistake that even the experts tell you to make is passing out multiple cards when networking. Instead, pass out a single card and only if asked for it.

Combat the Networking Mistake #1 ½: "Here is a card for you and one to pass on"

eTIFFANIE: Connect ONLINE with people you meet in person to begin building the "know, like" of "know, like, and trust."

Author's Note:

If your goal is to have people keep your business card and avoid the trash can:

eTIFFANIE: Invest in business cards that grab people's attention so they will be kept!

As you now know to give business cards only to people who ask for them, you have less need for lots of cards, and can invest in cards that are original. Whether you choose a unique shape, material, or add an eye-pleasing promotional item, make your card so memorable that people hesitate to discard them.
(For additional thoughts on unique or eye-catching business cards, visit *Bonus Material: Business Cards that Stick Around*.)

Networking Mistake #2: Wearing a Name Tag

"Hi, John," said Charlotte, glancing down at his name tag. "I see you are a Realtor," Charlotte says, thinking, my mother is a Realtor, my brother is a Realtor, I have my real estate license. Just why would I want to meet another real estate agent? How can I get out of this conversation quickly? "Pardon me; do you know where the restroom is?"

The experts share: Wear a name tag when networking.

Now you might be thinking, how could that be a mistake? The mistake here lies in *what you put on the name tag*.

As John and Charlotte's story epitomizes, many name tags actually can **hurt** you when networking. Studies do show that wearing a name tag makes you more approachable — and it does — so you will need one. Instead of sticking on a tag with the company name or logo, giving away your profession, be creative. We will explore what to put on your tag shortly.

Why wear a name tag?

Do be sure to wear a name tag while networking (though it is up to you if you wish to wear one when shopping at the grocery store or standing in line for coffee or at the bank as the tag can be a conversation starter).

For people who prefer not to, or think "everybody there already knows me," consider:

- Are there guests who may be in attendance?

- Have you ever been in an awkward situation, talking to someone who obviously knew you and is asking about your family, your favorite team, something that had recently happened in your life, and you cannot place that person's name?

- Did you ever want to introduce one person to another while networking and you could not recall the person's name? It would be really rude, and embarrassing, to ask for it again.
  Tip from the author: *When out with my husband, if I cannot remember a person's name, I introduce my spouse by saying, "This is my husband," who knows this cue means to shake the person's hand and offer his name. The other person typically responds with his or her name, and my credibility is saved.*

Simply wearing a name tag will help in all of the above situations.

There are various types of name tags you can wear to networking events. They range from the sticky "Hello, my name is…" tags, to professionally made tags that add to your credibility and usually cost between $10 and $20. If, like me, you occasionally misplace your name tag, purchase a couple and keep them handy, because you always want to have a name tag while networking.

What ought to be on your name tag?

The most popular type of name tag when networking includes the person's name as well as the company name and/or logo and is perfect to wear when hosting an event at your location or sponsoring an event. You want to be identifiable here. This name tag is also powerful when meeting with prospective clients, positioning you as a professional in a non-networking environment.

The problem with this name tag while networking is that people are going to associate you with your profession or company. These associations usually end the conversation instead of starting it.

Because your networking goal is to **book a meeting from the meeting** and you just ended the conversation (i.e., contemplate Charlotte and John's interaction above), the name tag did not help you!

The person reading your name tag assumes to know what you do based on previous experiences with others in your industry/field or company, and proceeds to put you in a preconceived box. If you are just like everyone else in your industry or company, this is okay. Most entrepreneurs, sales agents and sales professionals, especially the ones reading this book, have something that sets them apart from their competition, something that makes them unique.

Here's a real-life example of not judging a book by its cover: One of my favorite authors is Stephen King. I have read almost all of his books, some many times. When I talk to people about Stephen King, though, I often find people do not like his work. Knowing this, I ask if they have seen *The Shawshank Redemption* or *The Green Mile*, and usually, the answer is yes. I have found they almost always liked those movies. I then have the pleasure of surprising them by pointing out that both films were adapted from Stephen King novels.

Most people, when they think about Stephen King, think of some of his earlier movies; and even I will admit there are some bad Stephen King movies out there. For some, it was a few bad movies, and people conclude they have had enough of Stephen King. For others, they think of Stephen

King as horror and do not like that genre. They have judged the author by select pieces of his work.

When someone meets you for the first time at a networking event, and on your name badge is your company name and/or profession, you open yourself to the possibility that people will make an assumption about you based on what they know of others in your profession or company. Since you want to start instead of end the conversation, first share what makes you unique. How you do what you do (your profession) can come later.

Here, then, is the conundrum: You want to wear a name tag while networking, although one that's different. What can you do?

eTIFFANIE: Wear a CURIOSITY NAME TAG when networking!

The curiosity name tag's sole purpose is to have other people ask you about it. The advantage is, when asked, you get to tell the person asking **exactly what you do** instead of letting the person make assumptions about what you do.

The curiosity tag could be decorated with a word or short phrase, letters or graphics, visuals that get people wondering what your tag is all about and asking you about what you do.

One of my personal favorite name tags has my name followed by the letters MMST.

When I am networking, people come up to me and ask, "What's MMST?"

My response: "I help people <u>M</u>ake <u>M</u>oney and <u>S</u>ave <u>T</u>ime." When I share that, people look surprised, as if they were anticipating a longer, perhaps more pitchy answer (think elevator speech, which is another mistake, coming up next). My goal is to make the person I am talking to curious enough to ask how I make others money and save them time.

When asked, you now have permission to talk about what you do. If you are not asked, regrettably, it means the person is not really interested and just like with the business card, you do not offer any additional information.

As you are creating your curiosity name tag, give some thought as to what is going to be on the name tag and to a response that supports your tag and leaves the person wanting to know more about you and your business.

eTIFFANIE: Your name tag should START, not end, a conversation!

Let's look at a couple of examples:

ETOMORP - Rob Kellog is the owner of Thread Art, a company that specializes in helping companies make more money through promotional items and apparel. When someone asks about ETOMORP, Rob responds, "We help companies promote themselves, whether it be forward or backwards," while slowly sweeping his hand under the name tag so people see that etomorp is **promote** spelled backwards. "Whatever is best way to promote you, we will figure it out to help you profit!"

BNI - Tom Fleming supports more than 45 BNI chapters in West Central Florida; BNI is a networking organization that can help members increase their business through a structured, positive and professional program that enables them to develop long-term, meaningful relationships with quality business professionals. When asked what BNI stands for, Tom answers, "Bigger Net Income."

NIGHTS and WEEKENDS - Terri Scarcelli, the owner of Balanced Accounting, favors a name tag unusual for an accountant. She has images that symbolize nights and weekends. When asked about her name tag, she shares, "I help business owners take back their nights and weekends!"
She then shares how she helps professionals take back their nights and weekends instead of spending time on bookkeeping.

Each of these curiosity name tags helps to start a conversation, and ideally leads to questions like, "How do you do that?" or "Tell me more!"

You want to be creative when coming up with your curiosity name tag and your response to it. Be careful when crafting it, because the response you give is a teaser to see if people are interested in you, what you do, and how you help people.

Combat Networking Mistake #2: Wearing a Name Tag

eTIFFANIE: Wear a CURIOSITY NAME TAG when networking!

eTIFFANIE: Your name tag should START, not end, a conversation!

Networking Mistake #3: Use your Elevator Pitch

"Hi David, I'm Jackie," Jackie says, extending her hand. "What is it that you do?"

David, excited to share a pitch that he wrote, practiced, and perfected, takes a deep breath then shares: "Jackie, I am glad you asked! I sell widgets, and have been doing it for more than 10 years. My widgets are the best in..." As David continues to pitch to Jackie, she is wondering how long he can go on without taking a breath and how much he can cram into a single paragraph. She is abruptly drawn back when she hears David ask, "We can see which package would work best for you. What time are you available later this week?"

The experts share: Use your elevator pitch when networking.

Each expert will share with you "their" formula for the "perfect" elevator pitch and that is a mistake! While there is merit and value in having an elevator pitch, these speeches belong outside networking events, not during them.

The elevator pitch during a networking event is a mistake. Why?

An elevator pitch is selling to a room full of potential clients. The problem is most people do not attend networking events to buy!

When people go to a networking event to sell and no one is there to buy, a disconnect results. This is why many people feel that networking does not work, because they think networking is direct **prospecting**.

eTIFFANIE: Networking is not to be confused with prospecting, or selling.

These are wholly different activities.

The elevator pitch was originally designed so that if you were lucky enough to find yourself in the elevator with someone you wanted to sell to, you could pitch to them quickly. The ideal situation was a shared elevator going up or down several stories, giving enough time for the person to schedule a meeting from the conversation. It was used quite a bit in business as well as in Hollywood, where screenwriters hopped on elevators to pitch their scripts.

The elevator pitch is effective in pushing your product or service in less than a minute. As there should be no selling while networking, there is no place in networking for an elevator pitch.

eTIFFANIE: Ditch the elevator pitch when networking!

When networking and someone asks you what you do, how do you answer, if not with your pitch?

People commonly respond to "What do you do?" with a profession. If you remember the earlier mistake with name tags, what happens when you lead with your profession? Yep, you end right back in that box where people **assume** they know what you do. This effectively ends the conversation, instead of beginning it.

When networking, instead of trying to sell (elevator pitch) or putting yourself in a box (profession), use a funneling conversation.

"What's that?" you might ask. A funneling conversation is a series of questions used to determine if the person you are speaking to is a potential contact sphere relationship (non-competing industry with the same target market), a potential client, or neither.

Let's eavesdrop on a networking conversation between John and Sarah and, in dissecting the exchange, discover a funneling conversation:

"Hi, I'm John Smith," says John.
"Nice to meet you John. I am Sarah," says Sarah. "What is it that you do, John?"
John replies, "I am an architect."
"That sounds like fun," Sarah replies, and waits.
John then asks, "What it is that you do?"
Sarah, glad he asked, shares, "I work with entrepreneurs to help them make more money in less time!"
John, looking curious, asks, "Well, how do you do that?"
"Well, let me ask you John, are you currently looking to grow your business?"
John, nodding his head enthusiastically, replies, "I am! I am hoping to open a second office next year."
Sarah asks, "That's exciting. Would referrals help you make that happen?"
John, welcoming the prospect of growing his business, replies, "I love getting referrals. I find those are the best clients."
Sarah, smiles and asks, "So would doubling, tripling or even quadrupling your referrals help you out?"
*John, "Even doubling my referrals would have a **huge** impact."*

Sarah, "I work with people to help them greatly increase their referrals," Sarah briefly paused, "and I actually have a workshop coming up. If you are interested, perhaps I could get you a complimentary ticket for the event."

Of course, John says yes.

The funneling conversation, woven through their dialogue, helps determine if the other person is a potential client or if that person is a contact sphere referral source.

You know how to recognize your potential clients, let us explore the contact sphere relationship. A contact sphere relationship is the best potential source of referrals. Many people believe clients are the best referral sources, however they are not! Clients produce fewer referrals than contact sphere relationships, when properly educated and motivated.

eTIFFANIE: The best source of referrals are CONTACT SPHERE relationships, not clients.

While clients can be **powerful** referral sources, they lack the **contacts** of people in your target market (that group of people that has the greatest need for your product or service).

Contact sphere relationships are people who have the same target market as you, and are in a non-competing industry. These symbiotic relationships are able to pass along referrals consistently because of that shared target market.

When networking, a top priority is making contact sphere relationships so you can develop a referral relationship with them.

eTIFFANIE: When networking, search for potential contact sphere relationships in addition to potential clients.

It is up to you to know which professions best fit into your contact sphere, and the *Bonus Material* has a contact sphere section specifically to assist you.

Determining if the person you are speaking with is in your contact sphere is easy enough, as one of the first questions asked when networking usually uncovers this information.

If we revisit the exchange between John and Sarah, after the introductions, Sarah asked: *"What is it that you do, John?"*

When John replied he was an architect, Sarah asked herself, is that profession part of my contact sphere? For Sarah, the answer was no. Had an architect been a potential contact sphere relationship, her goal would then be to schedule a meeting **outside** of the networking event, so they would have the opportunity to begin to build the "know, like, and trust" foundation required for a referral relationship. Her request could be as simple as: "Wow, John, you are an architect? I actually find that I can pass referrals quite frequently to an architect. Would you be open to getting together so that I could learn more about your business? Maybe coffee, breakfast or lunch?"

The next meeting, outside of the networking event, would be to learn more about John and his potential as a referral partner. In the event of this meeting, do come prepared by researching the person online beforehand, using Google, the person's website and social media profiles (Facebook, Google+, LinkedIn, etc.).

For Sarah, unfortunately, John is not part of her contact sphere, and what she had to do next is one of the hardest parts of a networking conversation. She had to remain silent. She had to wait for John to ask, *"What is it that you do?"*

Had he not asked, he would have signaled that this may not be a reciprocal relationship, which puts Sarah in the simple position of moving on.

Luckily, John did ask, and instead of offering her profession or an elevator pitch, Sarah shared how she helps her clients.

eTIFFANIE: When asked "What do you do?", share how you HELP your clients.

In this case, Sarah shared, *"I work with entrepreneurs to help them make more money in less time!"* Then she paused again, waiting for John to request specifics. Once he asked for details, the **how** she does what she does, he gave her permission to continue the conversation.

This point is crucial, as most people will want to launch into the specifics of what they do, again leaving the other person to determine if you have a product/service worth purchasing. The power of the funneling conversation, conversely, is **you** asking the series of questions that determines if the other party is a prospect or not.

Let's re-examine Sarah and John's conversation:

"Well, let me ask you John, are you currently looking to grow your business?"
John, nodding his head enthusiastically replies, "I am! I am hoping to open a second office next year."
Sarah asks, "That's exciting. Would referrals help you make

that happen?"
John, welcoming the prospect of growing his business,
replies, "I love getting referrals. I find those are the best
clients."
Sarah smiles, and asks, "So would doubling, tripling or even
quadrupling your referrals help you out?"
John, "Even doubling my referrals would have a **huge**
impact."

Sarah asked a couple non-intrusive questions to determine if John was a potential client for her. If he had answered "no" at any point in the conversation above, then Sarah would have stopped asking questions. She now knows he is unlikely to become a client and could either say, "I help others who do have interest in expanding their business", move the conversation to another topic or exit gracefully (For advice on tactful exits, read *Networking Nugget #14: Exiting the Conversation Gracefully*).

Luckily for this example, and for Sarah, she got a "yes," which means she can now ask for the appointment. *"I work with people just like you to help them greatly increase their referrals, and I actually have a workshop coming up. If you are interested, perhaps I could get you a complimentary ticket for the event."*

Your "appointment" could be an invitation to an event, as in Sarah's case, or a meeting over coffee, or an initial consultation, both complimentary or paid.

As you can see, a conversation lasting a couple of minutes can yield amazing results by quickly determining if the person you are talking to is a contact sphere relationship, a prospect, or neither.

eTIFFANIE: Use the FUNNELING CONVERSATION to quickly determine if someone is a contact sphere relationship, a prospect, or neither.

Your funneling conversation is going to be a major time-saver and, more importantly, will allow you to qualify the prospect without preconceived notions of your profession coming into play. Do note, if the funneling conversation is "salesy" or unpracticed, it can be detrimental to your success. A funneling conversation should be conversational.
Practice, practice, practice!

The *Bonus Material* continues our exploration of funneling conversations, complete with examples and exercises to help you design your own and discover how you can use them to create many more referrals.

By utilizing this approach for introducing your profession or business when networking, you will be able to move quickly through the conversation and, if relevant, "book a meeting from a meeting." It eliminates long, drawn-out exchanges as you try to determine if someone is a good fit for you or not during an event where your goal is to meet many people versus a handful of people.

When done properly, the funneling conversation ends with a "yes" to the invitation you created and a satisfied prospective client walks away with a better understanding of the **benefits** of working with you and your business.

Combat Networking Mistake #3: Use your Elevator Pitch

eTIFFANIE: Networking is not to be confused with prospecting, or selling.

eTIFFANIE: Ditch the elevator pitch when networking!

eTIFFANIE: The best source of referrals are CONTACT SPHERE relationships, not clients.

eTIFFANIE: When networking, search for potential contact sphere relationships in addition to potential clients.

eTIFFANIE: When asked "What do you do?", share how you HELP your clients.

eTIFFANIE: Use the FUNNELING CONVERSATION to quickly determine if someone is a contact sphere relationship, a prospect, or neither.

Author's note:

As I began to write this book and deliver the material as a keynote presentation, I spent some time riding the elevator in business buildings.

I stood with my back to a side wall so I could look into the elevator during the ride. As people came on, I would ask them what floor they wanted, and press the button. Then, I would try to start up a conversation. Almost without exception, the person would avoid making any eye contact by looking at the floor, watching the change in floor levels, or staring at a smartphone. Most people were clearly not interested in conversing while we traveled up and down the building. Additionally, of the few people I began to have conversations with, not a single one asked what I do.

The elevator pitch I had prepared never got tested!

Networking Mistake #4: Networking to Grow your Business

Tommy wants to grow his business and his plan is to do it by getting referrals. He grabs his calendar and begins to schedule numerous networking events. Over the next several weeks, Tommy attends multiple events each day, meeting lots and lots of new people. At the end of the month, he sits back and looks at all the business cards he has collected, neatly arranged in stacks on his desk, and compares them to the referrals received from the same people. He has many business cards and very few referrals. Tommy wonders: "Where have I gone wrong? Why is networking not working for me?"

Too often, entrepreneurs like Tommy understand the importance of growing a business through referrals and think all they need to succeed is to attend networking events. Tommy networks and networks, meeting many new people, adding them to his ever growing database. Regrettably, networking and referral marketing are different activities even though the two often go hand-in-hand.

Networking can introduce you to people who have the potential to pass you referrals, however these are people you just met, meaning you are at the **beginning** of the "know, like and trust" relationship.

When the goal is to grow your business through referral marketing, you want to start with relationships already at the level of **trust**, instead of creating a large network of people you hardly know. Fortunately, you only need a handful of the **right relationships,** people who can pass you referrals **all day, every day,** to be truly successful.

While there are eight different types of referral sources (see: *Bonus Material: 8 Types of Referral Sources*), the sources to focus on are the **contact sphere** relationships, those who have the same clients you want and are in non-competitive professions, that already know, like and trust you.

Thinking about your network now, do you have relationships with the right people or do you need to start making them?

Here are three ways to fill the voids in your business network:

1. Network to meet the professionals you need. If you've read to this point, you are already familiar with the funneling conversation and can determine if someone has potential to be a part of your contact sphere.

2. Ask people already in your network to refer you to specific people or professions within your contact sphere, borrowing on the credibility you already have to make it happen.
   A sample conversation someone in your network could use to facilitate an introduction is: "If I could introduce you to a _____ (insert your profession here) that would have referrals for you over time, would you like to speak/meet with her/him?"

3. Cold Call. Since this is a book on networking and referrals, I am going to leave it at that.

eTIFFANIE: Fill the voids in your network by asking for referrals and connecting with the right people at networking events.

Knowing people in your contact sphere will result in a minimum of referrals. As you develop the relationship and move these people from "know" to "like" to **"trust,"** referrals will begin to flow abundantly between the two of you.

eTIFFANIE: You must build trust with people before they will refer you consistently.

How many contact sphere relationships do you want? With these relationships, more is better. As this group will become your referral TEAM (Together Everyone Achieves More), I recommend establishing referral relationships with at least nine to twelve people who work with your favorite clients. Each relationship will be unique; some will be *power performers*, while others will be great *team players*, offering occasional referrals.

There are two crucial components for moving a relationship from "know" to "like" to "trust," and achieving referral success: **motivation** and **education**. You will need to cultivate <u>both</u> to get to the point where referrals flow.

eTIFFANIE: Motivation and education are crucial components in building relationships that result in referrals.

Think back to Tommy, who attended countless networking events and gained very few referrals. He was adding people to his network, without motivating and educating them. He had little chance at success.

You can motivate your network by taking any number of steps. Here we explore *15 Ways to Strengthen your*

Referral Relationships (many are directly from the Certified Networker® Program):

1. **Send a note card**. A handwritten card is a steadfast way to create a lasting impression, especially when fewer and fewer people are utilizing this medium. A note card might be sent as a thank-you, for a birthday or upcoming holiday. Be sure to include a personalized message.
   (*Bonus Material: The Power of the Handwritten Card* contains additional hints on sending cards.)

2. **Send a gift**. A meaningful gift does not need to be expensive to have a powerful impact on your referral source. By matching the gift to the person's interests, you can create a memorable link to your source, as well as a motivated relationship.

3. **Call a Referral Source**. Take a few minutes to reach out with a simple "How are you doing?" to a key relationship in your network. The purpose of the call is merely to communicate and touch base. Try to call at a time convenient for your source.

4. **Offer a referral**. This is the most common way for people to motivate their referral sources, and there are different qualities of a referral that you can pass along. They range from offering a name and a phone number to bringing your referral partner to a closed deal. Referrals are powerful ways to encourage your source to respond in kind and thus strengthen the relationship. In making this referral to a prospect, also think of creating an introduction to a potential contact sphere relationship.

5. **Display a source's literature**. If you have an area open to the public, use it to share the collateral material of members of your business network to increase their visibility. Business cards, brochures and catalogs are just a few of the items that can be displayed.
   If you do not have a retail location, consider adding a link or two on your website to your referral sources' websites.

6. **Send an article of interest**. Passing along an article of interest to your referral source shows you are thinking about that person. The article, relevant to either his business or personal interests, can be shared in print or through electronic communication.

7. **Arrange a one-to-one meeting**. One of the most powerful ways to advance your relationship is sitting down to learn more about each other's business. Excel by asking questions, sharing successes and creating plans for promoting your businesses.

8. **Extend an invitation**. Invite your referral source to a networking event so you can introduce that person to others you know at the event, providing potential new business opportunities.

9. **Set up an activity**. Pick an activity you and your referral source enjoy, for example fishing, golfing, a sporting event, or pedicures, and get to know each other in an informal setting. Perhaps arrange a barbecue or lunch with a group of people and create introductions.

10. **Nominate a referral source**. Taking the time to nominate a source for an award or recognition can be a powerful way to help that person build visibility and credibility, while displaying your respect for that professional. Be sure, though, to let your source know you initiated the nomination.

11. **Include a source in your literature**. Having a newsletter or blog can be a powerful tool for building your own brand and using it to spotlight your sources increasing their reach as well. A few ways you can include a source are: shine a spotlight by giving a testimonial to sources, offering a coupon for their products/services, sharing an article they wrote, or linking to their website.

12. **Promote a source on social media**. Promotion on social media exposes your source to all the people connected with you on each of your networks. Build the source's credibility by offering success stories and your personal testimony.

13. **Arrange a speaking engagement**. An invitation to speak to the right group is an invaluable opportunity for your referral source to showcase his or her expertise and promote the business. Help arrange the engagement to a roomful of potential clients.

14. **Endorse their product or service**. The #1 objective in your referral marketing campaign is to have others speaking positively on your behalf; motivate your referral sources by offering written and video testimonials for their companies, or helping solicit one from a client. An effective

testimonial speaks to how a source best serves their clients.

15. **Offer Referral Incentives and Rewards**.
    Rewarding people when you receive a referral or close a referral increases the likelihood you will be referred again. Referral incentives are packed with bonuses, inspiring people to give you additional referrals.

Once people in your network are motivated, they also will need to be educated, as these two go hand-in-hand, and you cannot have one without the other. How do you educate your sources, and give them the tools and know-how they need to help you grow your business?

Here are just a few, out of many, topics you may want to teach your referral sources about you to make it easier for them to pass you referrals:

- **Why you do what you do.** Distinguish yourself from your competition by being able to clearly articulate what drives the passion you have for the work you do. For additional information, I recommend you attend the Certified Networker® Program, which includes a section titled, Emotionally Charged Connection®, your story of the how and why behind your business.

- **Target Market**. Who is your ideal client, the person or business you are looking to work with? Explaining clearly and succinctly your target market also teaches your network exactly which referrals you want — and those you don't want.
  (*Bonus Material: Contact Sphere* offers information about determining your Target Market.)

- **Triggers**. It is important to know what your prospects are saying and doing **before** they are ready to do business with you. While we would like people to ask for us by name, training our network with the buzzwords people use when in the market for our product or service opens the potential to doing business with more people than those who might already know us.

  For example, for an event planner, a trigger could be a new engagement ring or a woman talking her recent engagement. These triggers lead to the next point...

- **Conversation Starters**. These questions, or series of questions, are important when it comes to referrals. You can guide the exchange with conversation starters, questions that help you determine if there is a need or serious desire for your product/service. For example, with our event planner, the conversation starter might be: "Congratulations! Do you know when/where you are planning to get married?" You will want to warn your referral sources who see or hear a trigger of yours not to pounce on the unsuspecting prospect, trying to create the referral then and there.

- **Funneling Conversation.** We can educate our referral sources how to generate referrals for us by teaching them our funneling conversation.

  This has been explored in Networking Mistake #3, as well as you can also see *Bonus Material: Funneling Conversation* for help on creating your own.

- **How to Overcome Objections**. We hear "no" all the time; it's just part of doing business. If our referral sources are willing to create business on our behalf, they, too, need to know how to overcome the "no's" certain to come their way. If not, they may tire of those "no's" and stop trying altogether. Ensure that your referral sources know what to say in overcoming the most common objections you receive from prospective clients, which likely are focused around time, money, or both.

- **Referral Preferences.** This piece of information is crucial for your referral partners, as they need to know how you want to be referred.
  Do you want permission to be called, or are you looking for an appointment and a face-to-face introduction? Do you only accept check, or will a credit card do?
  Be confident in the kind of referral you want. For years, I would take a name and phone number and then chase people around, trying to make an appointment. I found that when I asked my TEAM for face-to-face introductions, I was much more likely to close the business and save time for the prospect and myself. Teach your team how to refer you the *right way*.

- **Success Stories/Testimonials**. I saved the best for last, although I almost topped the list with success stories.
  In order to arm your team with testimonials, you must first gather success stories from your clients. Have clients detail their delight at your products or services, telling how amazing you are at what you do. Common objections heard in your line of work also can be addressed here, so get testimonials from clients that can help overcome those objections. Once you have collected the testimonials, arm your team with the success stories so they will be able to

articulate how you have helped your clients. These success stories are **powerful** and can motivate referrals still on the fence to do business with you.

Training your TEAM with a couple of these topics will help your network on the path of what they need to know to refer you more!

Identify and build relationships with people in your contact sphere, motivate and educate those people, and be prepared for the referrals to flow in and watch your business flourish!

Combat Networking Mistake #4: Networking to Grow your Business

eTIFFANIE: You must build trust with people before they will refer you consistently.

eTIFFANIE: Motivation and education are crucial components in building relationships that result in referrals.

As we take a look back at the *4½ Networking Mistakes* that even the experts tell you to make, realize the key is simply being more effective with your networking time and creating the success you truly desire.

By only giving your cards to people who ask, you are working on moving forward those relationships that have the best potential for business, eliminating unnecessary follow-up.

By wearing a curiosity name tag, you encourage the conversation to **start** instead of end, and by pairing your introductions with a funneling conversation, you are able to quickly see if the person you are speaking to is a contact sphere relationship, a prospect, or neither.

Once you have the **right** relationships, work to strengthen them outside the networking event by educating and motivating them, creating **Referral Partners**, people who can pass you Referrals for Life®!

19 Networking Nuggets

The *4½ Networking Mistakes* that even the experts tell you to make were the inspiration for this book. In addition, what follows are 19 Networking Nuggets that will set you on the way to being a **master networker**, growing your business by referral.

These 19 Networking Nuggets have been gathered from the "10 Commandments of Networking a Mixer", from the Certified Networker® Program, fellow master networkers from around the world, as well as from inside my head, and compiled here for more productive networking by you!

Networking events might be breakfasts, lunches, coffees, after-hour mixers, open houses, or lunch-and-learns, and while each opportunity is different, some events emphasize business while others swing toward the social end of the spectrum. Regardless of type or focus, the goal is to add structure to what is often an unstructured environment, enabling you to make money and save time by efficiently networking.

The Networking Nuggets are broken into four sections:

- Before the Event

- Dealing with Networking Nervousness

- During the Event

- After the Event

I hope you use these nuggets to be more powerful and purposeful when networking!

Before the Event

Networking Nugget #1: Pick the Right Networking Event

Networking events are like ice cream: they all are made up of the same basic ingredients and have the same texture, even though each group and event has its own flavor. Before you begin networking, you need to determine where you will find events that are the right events for you.

You can network anytime, anywhere: at expos or trade shows, community happenings, get-togethers initiated at MeetUp.com, or the most popular forum — events arranged by organizations.

A number of different organizations offer mixers, meetings, or lunches for their members. Some of the most popular are:

- **Chambers of Commerce.** The Chamber of Commerce is one of the largest service groups, literally spanning the world. Within in the United States, each county or city may have its own Chamber of Commerce. The focus of each varies, from the community to business or the economy, as do the events each chamber hosts. These might range from a meal with a guest speaker to after-hour mixers and even ribbon cuttings.

- **BNI.** BNI is the largest strong-contact networking organization in the world. Strong-contact networking groups allow only one person per profession as a member to their weekly meetings, where the focus is on members passing referrals. BNI offers a structured, professional word-of-mouth program to help develop long-term, meaningful relationships. Find the chapter nearest you at www.BNI.com.

- **Community Service Clubs.** There are amazing service clubs, like Rotary, Kiwanis, or Lions, that focus on helping advance the community. These groups can be a great place to meet the local movers and shakers. Because these clubs focus on giving back and the community, be careful not to overly load a conversation with business.

- **Women's Associations.** Women's groups were created for the purpose of networking with like-minded women in a response, of sorts, to good ole boys clubs. Like the Chambers of Commerce, different groups have a different focus. Do note the majority of women's groups welcome men.

- **Professional Associations.** As expected, these are associations built around a particular profession. Depending on your industry, with care you may be able to turn competition into collaboration and create referrals from this group. Additionally, you may want to inquire into professional organizations based around your target market or contact sphere.

Where you network is essential for your success or failure when networking. Before attending an event, do establish whether people in your target market or contact sphere are likely to attend. If not, perhaps you should find another event.

Networking Nugget #2: Have Your Networking Tools with You at All Times

This networking nugget, along with a few to follow, is inspired by the "10 Commandments of Networking a Mixer". I first experienced these 10 commandments in 2006, while a student at the Certified Networker® Program offered by the Referral Institute®. These commandments were created by Dr. Ivan Misner and can be found in their entirety in "The World's Best Known Marketing Secret,"

There are a few tools you always want to have with you to most productively work a networking event. These include:

- **A Curiosity Name Tag**

- **Business Cards.** As a serious professional focused on growing your business by referral, you want to have more than enough business cards available for each event. Leave extras in your car, pocket, bag, etc., as a guarantee.

- **Calendar.** Your goal is to book the meeting from the meeting, which means scheduling a follow-up meeting right away instead of trading emails and phone calls later. Carry your calendar to make this easier, whether it is a paper calendar or an electronic one.

- **Writing Instrument.** Have a pen or pencil to take notes with and schedule appointments. A silver Sharpie is a particularly good choice because it will write on almost every business card.

- **Breathe Mints/Gum.** Make sure people will want to speak to you instead of running away! A healthy alternative is peppermint oil; a few drops will refresh your breath.

- **A Smile.** Be approachable by always displaying a great smile and positive attitude. If you are having a bad day, fake it 'til you make it or just stay away!

I recommend storing these necessities in a single place in your car, perhaps with backups (just in case), so your networking tools are always with you.

Networking Nugget # 3: Create a Goal

Oftentimes, people at networking events turn their focus to distractions, like: "How much longer do I have to stay?" "Where is the food?" and "Where is the bar?" Whereas if you walk in knowing exactly how many and what type of people you want to meet, you can leave once the goal is accomplished.

Which goals might you keep in mind when networking?

- Booking meetings with prospects and potential referral sources.

- Inviting people to relevant events.

- Connecting and reconnecting with people you already know, possibly by scheduling follow-up meetings.

You can be proactive in reaching your goal of meeting new people quickly. Try connecting with the host of the event or the person working the front door to ask guidance in finding the right type of people for you. Some events also post their guest lists online before the event starts.

Set your goals, work the room, and generate the success you are looking for!

Before the Event:

Networking Nugget # 1: Pick the Right Networking Event

Networking Nugget #2: Have Your Networking Tools with You at All Times

Networking Nugget #3: Create a Goal

Dealing with Networking Nervousness

I would consider myself to be a masterful networker; at the same time, I am an introvert. Walking into a room packed with 50 to 100 people is enough to have those nerves come out! We know we need to network, and can often feel overwhelmed, uncomfortable, and confused as to where to start. Yet, inside that room may be the ideal referral partner, rewarding client, or the perfect solution to a pressing problem.

Luckily, a couple of gentlemen taught me four great tips to deal with such fear, and I have asked them to share these tips with you. Ready?

Networking Nugget #4: Act Like a Host, not a Guest
From Dr. Ivan Misner, founder and CVO (Chief Visionary Officer) of BNI

When you are a guest at an event, you are often left waiting on others to make things happen and required to go with the flow. When you are the **host**, you create the event you want, know where to sign-in, or essentials like food and beverages, and make sure people are comfortable and introduce them around. By acting as the host, your visibility and credibility will skyrocket.

As a host, you want to:

- Make sure no guests are left unattended

- Create introductions

- Help people with the layout of the room (check-in, locating sponsor tables, food and beverage, restrooms, etc.)

Acting like the host is an ideal way to refine or develop excellent networking skills and engage with greater numbers of entrepreneurs in a shorter amount of time. The credibility created also may help in getting those referrals to flow.

You may have to "fake it 'til you make it" to become comfortable acting as host at events you attend. If you are unable to fake it, volunteer to be an ambassador or visit host for networking organizations you already belong to.

Ivan Misner, Ph.D., is a New York Times best-selling author, and the Founder of BNI (www.BNI.com), the world's largest business networking organization.

Networking Nugget #5: Tag-Team Networking
By Tom Fleming, BNI Executive Director & Referral Institute Trainer in West Central Florida

Dwight Davies and Bob Roberts often attend networking events together. Dwight runs a local marketing consulting firm and Bob is a prominent realtor in the area. At one event, Dwight recognized a woman from the law firm of Smith, Bernstein & Kawolski from the advertising her firm does in the community. This particular firm has a great reputation around town as really taking care of its clients, of keeping their best interests at heart.

As Dwight and Bob casually made it over to the professionally dressed woman, Dwight slowly took a step forward, held out his hand, and, glancing at her name badge, said, *"Fran, I would like you to meet Bob Roberts of Roberts Realty. Possibly you have met before?"* Fran smiled and shared, *"I don't think so."* Dwight continued, *"Bob comes from a broken home and knows how tough separation and divorce can be on families. Bob specializes in working with such families on their housing needs, and all their needs, for that matter, thrown into crisis due to separation and divorce. I know your firm has a great reputation in town as Family Law specialists who really care about their clients, too."*

Bob then took a step forward and shared, "Yes, it's great to finally meet someone from your firm, Fran. I have been looking to meet someone from Smith, Bernstein & Kawolski due to the caring reputation you all have earned. How have you come to develop that reputation?"

Fran shared a bit of the firm's history as Dwight and Bob remained fully engaged in the conversation.

Bob then shared, "I'm sorry Fran. I haven't introduced Dwight. Have you met before, by chance?" Again Fran smiled, looked Dwight in the eye, and shook her head no. Bob went on to share that Dwight runs a marketing firm in town and mentioned a couple of his prominent clients. She acknowledged having seen some of his work in various local publications, of hearing talk of him on radio spots, and of being friends with some of his clients via social media. Fran was excited to meet Dwight and asked for his card. Evidently the firm, just the previous week, had let its current marketing firm go. Fran promised to reach out to Dwight the next week to discuss the marketing message the firm is looking to promote and their thoughts on media strategy.

As the conversation neared its end, Dwight shared with Fran that he would love to see she and Bob get together, given that Fran's clients have housing needs fitting Bob's expertise. Dwight shared with Fran how Bob has worked for years helping hundreds of people caught in delicate situations like separation and divorce. Fran agreed that Bob would indeed be a great resource. She offered to accept a phone call to set up a meeting and explore how he might best support the clients of Smith, Bernstein & Kawolski.

Great story, was sheer luck or superb strategy at play?

It's always about strategy, intentionally applied.
In this instance, "tag-team networking".

Let's look at what just happened.

Dwight and Bob have had a great business relationship for a while. They are confident in each other's services and comfortable referring one another. They have taken the time to get to know each other's style, each other's stories, each other's target markets and referral relationships. Each knows how to promote the other; how to sell for one another.

Dwight and Bob also understand the power of a testimonial, of someone else promoting your product or service. If Bob had approached Fran and shared, "My name's Bob and I am the Realtor you should be referring all of your clients to," the conversation would have ended there. Whenever we are telling people how great we are or how great our products and services are, we are selling. Let's face it, no one likes to be sold to!

Dwight and Bob are masterful at supporting one another. They pick up a guest list in advance of events they attend, review it, and target specific people to whom they each want to be introduced.

Networking can be intentional. In fact, networking should be intentional, because intentional networking is both effective and efficient.

Tom is a master trainer for the Referral Institute® and featured on "Who Can Pass You Business All Day Every Day", an audio CD that focuses on helping people create referrals, all day, every day!

A thought from the author on this Networking Nugget: *When I am picking who I want to network with me, I first think of my networking challenges and find someone who can help me move beyond them. I am an introvert (which often surprises people) and it takes effort to walk up to people I do not know and strike up a conversation. So, before networking events, I look for extroverts who enjoy speaking to everyone, pair up, and allow them to "break the ice" on my behalf with Tag Team Networking.*

Networking Nugget #6: Arrive Early
By Phil Bedford, Master Franchisor of Referral Institute, Middle East

By being among the first people to arrive to a networking event, you can skip potentially uncomfortable entrances and discover a couple of hidden benefits.

Let the room fill around you
By arriving early, you allow people to trickle in around you, slowly filling up of the room around you. This approach is less stressful on you, and certainly better

than walking into a jumbled mess. Plus, should you start to feel truly uncomfortable in the crowd, you can leave with a clear conscience; chances are, by then you have already met those you had set as your goal of introducing yourself.

Help the Organizer

Often the organizers can be overwhelmed with things to do. Pitching in is often a way you can help gain credibility with them. Not only will the help be appreciated, you also get the chance to meet some of the more connected people there who, in turn, may end up connecting you with others.

Wait by the registration desk

There will be many guests who are nervous. By positioning yourself by the sign in desk, you can act like one of the hosts of the event and make people feel welcome. Being the first smiling face someone sees already gets you off to the right start. Taking the lead at check-in or with picking up name badges allows you to spot people of interest to you, and slip in a "hello."

Phil Bedford, who also is known as the Rebel Networker (www.rebelnetworker.tv), is a Master Trainer for the Referral Institute® in the Middle East.

Networking Nugget #7: Approach People in Open Two's and Three's

By Dr. Ivan Misner, founder and CVO (Chief Visionary Officer) of BNI

Entrepreneurs attending networking events often have a difficult time reading the crowd and knowing when and where to get started. Sometimes this is their biggest challenge in networking. They may be thinking: "I don't want to just barge in. Where do I start? Who do I talk to?"

Being able to assess a room is an important skill. For example, look at Diagram A, below. Here is a top-down view of a portion of a room during a business mixer. For the person entering the room (below, individual with the "?" in the bottom-right corner), it's hard to determine where to start in the networking process.

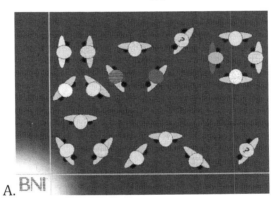

A. BNI

With that in mind, consider this. The next time you are attending a networking mixer, take note of how people are physically grouped together. You will find that people stand with their bodies clearly indicating whether or not they are open to having someone approach and join them. In other words, literally look for "open" vs. "closed" groups.

What do I mean by open vs. closed groups? Compare the two diagrams below. You will note that in Diagram B, the two people are standing parallel to one another with their shoulders squared off in a way that does not make it easy for anyone to enter the conversation. It is a Closed Two group. However, in Diagram C, note that the two parties are standing slightly askew, which makes it easier for someone to join the conversation. This is an example of an Open Two.

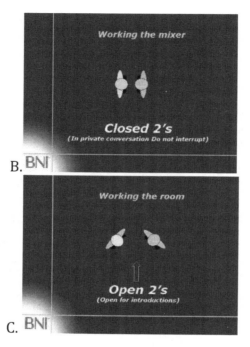

B.

C.

In Diagram D, below, you will see an example of a Closed Three group. In this illustration, you can see they have closed the circle, thus indicating they are having a more private conversation or are not interested in meeting someone else. This would **not** be the group to break into and then introduce yourself.

Sometimes the Closed Three's do open for a time, and then re-close. As you watch the group, take the opportunity to come in the group during the times when they are physically open. This usually indicates the ebb and flow of conversation, and lets you know there is a break in the intensity of conversation, or at least in the privacy of the conversation.

On the other hand, look at Diagram E. In this illustration, you can clearly see there is room for another person to join in the group. The Open Three's stand with a slight break between two of them.

These "open" configurations are what to look for in groups of business people you don't know.

.

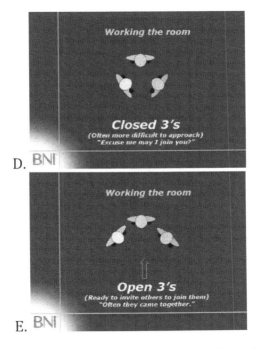

D. BNI

E. BNI

Being able to read a crowd, any size crowd, and gauge when to come in to a group of two, three, or more people who are networking is an acquired skill. If you struggle with this concept, you might be destined to attend event after event before finally making the presumption that networking events are not a good way for you to make connections or develop new networking partners.

This could not be further from the truth. You must put yourself into the mix for it to work. I like to say, "Networking is a contact sport." In order to make those connections, you need to successfully gauge the warmth of the smaller gatherings of people at the mixer.

Below is Diagram A again. Take another look at it. Can you spot the open and closed groups? It's amazing how the same diagram makes sense when you look at it from the perspective of open or closed groups.

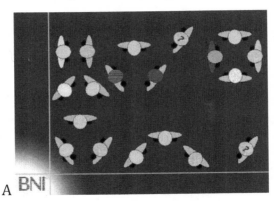

A BNI

Often people who attend the mixer together will stay grouped together for the entire event. As the event unfolds, however, they will open and close their grouping. I have seen this happening and watched as networkers who were savvy to this concept came into the grouping as it opened, met the attendees, and then moved around the room meeting others, collecting business cards of future contacts for their successful networking efforts.

By utilizing the analogy of Open and Closed Three's, you should find that the next networking mixer you attend will be more profitable as well as more enjoyable!

In Dr. Misner's book, "Networking Like a Pro," which can be viewed at www.IvanMisner.com, he shares how to approach people.

Dealing with Networking Nervousness

Networking Nugget #4: Act Like a Host, not a Guest

Networking Nugget #5: Tag-Team Networking

Networking Nugget #6: Arrive Early

Networking Nugget #7: Approach People in Open Two's and Three's

During the Event

There are several things you can do during networking events to maximize your energy and efforts.

Networking Nugget #8: Utilize your Funneling Conversation

When asked "What do you do?", respond with your funneling conversation.
Remember, at the back of the book is *Bonus Material: Creating your Funneling Conversation* to help create your own funneling conversation.

Networking Nugget #9: Offer Support to Others

When first meeting someone at an event, you have an opportunity to be truly memorable. Seize hold by extending your support.

The level of support worth offering depends on the needs presented. Be creative in how you assist; in supporting people in their success, you are building your credibility quickly.

What types of support could we offer? A few examples are:

- Invite the person to another event

- Introduce that person to others at the event

- Share information about networking organizations you belong to, and encourage him to visit with you

- Follow up with an article or link for a specific issue/concern the person is facing

- Create a referral to a member of your network, should the person you just met have a need for the particular product/service

By supporting people you meet *quickly*, you will be remembered in a positive way. One day, these people may well return the favor by offering you support, perhaps even in the form of a referral.

Networking Nugget #10: Listen and Ask Questions (5W+H)

As Dale Carnegie shared, showing a genuine interest by truly listening to the person you are speaking with can help forge a relationship. You gain information through such interest, a powerful tool in moving the relationship forward. The details you learn also help in determining if you want to schedule a meeting with that person.

In conjunction with listening, you may want to use the mirroring technique to ask people questions you wish them to ask you. Politely inquiring, "Who is your ideal client?" significantly increases the odds of being asked the same in return.

Common networking questions include:

- Why do you do what you do?

- Who is your ideal client?

- Which professions pass you frequent referrals?

- When did you get into business? Or, how long have you been in business?
- Where else do you network?
- What areas do you work in?
- How do you differ from your competition?
- Do you have any specials?

Please note you will want a dazzling answer at the ready if you get asked that same question!

Networking Nugget #11: Exchange Business Cards when Asked

Recall:
eTIFFANIE: When networking, give out your business card ONLY when you are asked!

Avoid **in-person spamming** and remember the purpose of exchanging business cards is so you are able to follow up with people after the networking event, to continue building the relationship.

Networking Nugget #12: Take Notes on the Back of Business Cards You Collect

During a networking event, you will have the opportunity to meet many new people, and unless you have an eidetic memory, you may have trouble remembering all the details. Taking notes on the back of business cards ensures that pertinent information is captured in writing. This could include when and where you met the person, distinct attributes (very tall or British accent), the nature of the referral (ideal or a possibility), support offered, and follow-up activities necessary to make certain your goals are reached. These notes will be useful for follow-up and should be added to the notes section of your database.

Before writing on the back of a business card, do ask permission. In some cultures, such an action is an insult to the person who gave you the card.

Many business cards today are packed with information and images and coated on both sides, making them hard to write on. A silver metallic Sharpie can take notes on 99% of business cards and makes a great addition to your networking kit. An alternative is to keep a small sticky notepad handy, jotting down notes and then sticking them to the card.

Networking Nugget #13: Spend Less Than 5 Minutes with Each Person You Meet

Too often when networking, people have a tendency to meet a potential client or referral source and spend all their time speaking with that person. Remember, the goal of attending a networking event is to **book a meeting from the meeting**, reaching the goals set for yourself with Networking Nugget #3: Set a Goal for the Number and Type of People You Want to Meet. When you find someone who interests you, with the potential to be a client or referral source, immediately book the next meeting then move on, meeting additional people until you have reached your goal.

Also avoid trying to close business deals; it is impractical and **networking and selling do not mix**. You may be able to increase sales to a hot prospect by taking the time to schedule another meeting to fully discuss a range of needs.

The best way to follow this Networking Nugget, and keep your conversations under 5 minutes, is to utilize the funneling conversation. You will be surprised at how easy it is to quickly move through a conversation when you go into a networking event with **intention**.

A frequent challenge is ending the conversation, which leads us to the next Networking Nugget.

Networking Nugget #14: Exit the Conversation Gracefully

Many networkers find themselves stuck with that one person who just wants to keep talking, making it hard to leave. Why? Likely reasons are the person is shy and feels comfortable speaking to you, the person sees you as a powerful prospect and really wants to sell to you, or they are unaware the conversation has naturally ended.

In ending a conversation with someone, be honest and polite, if only because you may run into that person again, in business or in life. In fact, a good rule of thumb is to always exit a conversation with grace, anticipating you will be speaking with that person again soon.

Let's first examine a few ways **not** to leave a conversation:

- "Oh, I see somebody really important who I need to talk to." Besides making the person feel small and unimportant, this hurts your credibility.

- Walk off in the middle of a sentence.

- Pretend to get an important text or phone call. This impacts your credibility, as you should be there to network and it may leave people wondering about your priorities should they refer a client to you.

- Point over their shoulder and yell, "Dilapidated ostrich" and run away. (Thanks to my younger brother Robert for this suggestion.)

Now, here are a few approaches for leaving a conversation gracefully:

- "It has been really great speaking with you this evening. I know you are looking to meet other people here, and I want to give you time to do so. I do hope to see you again soon," and then, having politely wrapped up the conversation, you move on to the next person.

- Introduce the person to someone at the event who would be a good connection, either a prospect or contact sphere relationship.

- "I see that _____ (insert person's name) has just come free, and I have been trying to catch him/her all night. Will you excuse me?"

- Refresh yourself with food or a beverage.

- Excuse yourself to go to the restroom. (Caveat: Ladies, I have been followed into the restroom by the person I was speaking to on more than one occasion using this excuse. Definitely awkward.)

- If all else fails, having a wingman at the event to send a secret rescue signal works wonders.

Choose whichever one or a combination of these tips that will work best for you, and stay **focused** on your networking goals!

Networking Nugget #15: Avoid Spending Time with People You Already Know

While it is great to catch up with people you know, you are missing the opportunity to engage with **potential** clients and referral partners.

Networking Nugget #16: Remember the Platinum Rule®

For generations, people have been taught the Golden Rule: treat others the way you want to be treated. The problem, though, is that not everyone wants to be treated as you do. Instead, practice the Platinum Rule®, "Treat others the way they want to be treated," as coined by Dr. Tony Alessandra (*Tony Alessandra is an American best-selling author, entrepreneur and motivational speaker, with an expertise in behavioral styles*).

When networking, your ability to adapt to others and treat them as they want to be treated will result in a much more comfortable conversation, easing nervousness on both sides.

For more information on adapting to others and using the Platinum Rule®, please visit *Bonus Material: Behavioral Styles.*

Networking Nugget #17: Avoid the Networking Don'ts

Avoid awkward situations when networking. Don't:

- Sell.

- Network with a bad or negative attitude. Paste a smile on your face, fake it 'til you make it. If you are unable to shake a sour mood, then you are better off not networking.

- Drink too much. Networking is about moving relationships from **know** to **like** to **trust**, and you do not want to start off on the wrong foot by overindulging.

- Forget the deodorant.

- Try to make yourself look better by talking poorly about your competition. While you may succeed at disgracing your competitor, you are no longer that attractive either.

- Use inappropriate language or humor. Keep your commentary G or PG.

- Steer clear of controversial topics, including politics and religion.

- Correct the person, even if they may be wrong. True story, with name changed to protect the ignorant, I meant innocent!

My husband, Rob, had met a professional, Mr. D, while networking. They exchanged information, and then went their separate ways. A couple months later, Rob received a request for Mr. D's service. That same day, Rob saw Mr. D at another networking event. Excited to pass the referral to Mr. D, Rob approached him. Mr. D introduced himself, and when Rob said, "I believe we have already met," Mr. D denied this, twice. Rob walked away, the referral undelivered.

Rob, by the way, recommends telling people "Nice to see you" instead of "Nice to meet you," in case you don't recall having met before.

- Pass out large collateral material, such as catalogs, flyers, or books. When networking, people are not looking to hold onto bulky pieces. While you may want to have catalogs on hand if used in your business, pass them out, only if asked.

During the Event

Networking Nugget #8: Utilize your Funneling Conversation

Networking Nugget #9: Offer Support to Others

Networking Nugget #10: Listen and Ask Questions (5W+H)

Networking Nugget #11: Exchange Business Cards when Asked

Networking Nugget #12: Take Notes on the Back of Business Cards You Collect

Networking Nugget #13: Spend Less Than 5 Minutes with Each Person You Meet

Networking Nugget #14: Exit the Conversation Gracefully

Networking Nugget #15: Avoid Spending Time with People You Already Know

Networking Nugget #16: Remember the Platinum Rule®

Networking Nugget #17: Avoid the Networking Don'ts

By remembering and using these 10 Networking Nuggets during a networking event, you will be able to more competently work the event and reach your goals!

After the Event

As previously discussed in *4½ Networking Mistakes*, networking by itself is not enough.

eTIFFANIE: It's what happens AFTER the networking event, not during, that leads to true referral success!

The last two networking nuggets guide you in what to do after the event.

Networking Nugget #18: Follow Up

Communicating with prospective clients and sources outside of the event is necessary, even essential. Whether sending promised information, scheduling or confirming an appointment, or simply just staying in touch, make sure to follow up with emergent relationships. Doing so in a timely manner is crucial. Even if you lack follow-up material to offer, quickly dropping a reminder of an appointment will show your professionalism and build your credibility.

Many people wonder, what is the **best way to follow up**? Here are three ways to answer that question:

- **A handwritten note**. This blast from the past is something very few people do anymore and its impact is **amazing**. When was the last time you received a handwritten note from a person you met when networking?
One disadvantage to a handwritten note, though, is

that it is hardly a form of two-way communication; when following through on plans made at a networking event, you likely still need to make a call or send an email.

(Three key components for creating powerful, handwritten cards are in *Bonus Material: The Power of the Handwritten Card.*)

- **Consistency**. If you prefer to reach out with a phone call, then this is your ideal follow-up method. If email is the only way you communicate, utilize it. The best method for you is whichever one you are most comfortable with and can do every time the need arises.

- **The Platinum Rule®**. How a potential relationship would prefer a follow-up may be one of the questions to ask when networking. Keep in mind the Platinum Rule®: "Treat others the way THEY want to be treated." By adapting to the other's preference, you will increase your likelihood of being referred. Typically, by behavioral style, know that: Go-Getters and Examiners prefer email while the Nurturer and Promoters prefer a phone call. (See *Bonus Material: Behavioral Styles.*)

Pick which method works best for you, and be sure to **follow up!**

Think back to Networking Nugget #3: Create a Goal for the number and type of people you want to meet. Taking it a step further, remember to create your goal based on the amount of time in your calendar for follow-up. If you have three appointments available over the coming weeks, then your goal for an event is three meetings with prospects/referral sources. By scheduling follow-up time into networking events, you guarantee having sufficient time to do both effectively and grow your business by referral.

Schedule time to meet with referral sources and prospects, as well as to follow up with notes, emails, or phone calls.

Networking Nugget #19: Connect Online to Strengthen Offline Relationships

Networking gives you the chance to meet new people; connecting online after the initial meeting further develops the "**know, like**" components necessary for a referral relationship.

Scan social media sites you are active on for the people you have just met and, if they are also members, connect with them. Communicating online in this way will keep your name (and photo) literally before their eyes, increasing the likelihood they will think of you when the need arises.

(For tips on maximizing your online networking, see *Bonus Material: Taking Networking Online.*)

After the Event:

Networking Nugget #18: Follow Up

Networking Nugget #19: Connect Online to Strengthen Offline Relationships

I hope these 19 Networking Nuggets are helpful in your continued networking success. Thank you for joining me on this journey!

Networking Nuggets

Before the event
#1: Pick the Right Networking Event
#2: Have Your Networking Tools with You at All Times
#3: Create a Goal

Dealing with Networking Nervousness
#4: Act Like a Host, not a Guest
#5: Tag-Team Networking
#6: Arrive Early
#7: Approach People in Open Two's and Three's

During the Event
#8: Utilize your Funneling Conversation
#9: Offer Support to Others
#10: Listen Well and Ask Questions (5W+H)
#11: Exchange Business Cards when Asked
#12: Take Notes on the Backs of Business Cards You Collect
#13: Spend Less Than 5 Minutes with Each Person You Meet
#14: Exit the Conversation Gracefully
#15: Avoid Spending Time with People You Already Know
#16: Remember the Platinum Rule®
#17: Avoid the Networking Don'ts

After the Event
#18: Follow up
#19: Connect Online to Strengthen Offline Relationships

Section Three: Bonus Material

Throughout the book, I wanted to provide more in-depth information on select topics and working instructions for tools you want to master, like funneling conversations. Additionally, I wanted to keep a nice and easy flow throughout the book, therefore I developed the Bonus Material here in third section.

I hope this bonus material is helpful!

Bonus Material:

- Determining your Contact Sphere

- Creating your Funneling Conversation

- 8 Types of Referral Sources

- Arming your Staff to Pass Referrals

- Creative Business Cards

- Behavioral Styles, by Dawn Lyons

- The Power of the Handwritten Card, by Paula Bonnell

- Taking Networking Online, by Courtney Nestler

Bonus Material: Determining your Contact Sphere

As you now know, contact sphere relationships are professionals that have the same target market as you and are in a non-competing industry. These symbiotic relationships are able to pass you referrals consistently because of that shared target market!

This group holds the **most potential** of your eight referral sources as these people deal with your ideal clients each and every day! (For the other seven sources, see *Bonus Material: 8 Different Kinds of Referral Sources.*)

The first step in determining which professions make up your contact sphere is knowing your target market. Entrepreneur.com defines a target market as, "a specific group of consumers at which a company aims its products and services".

While this sounds rather straight-forward, many entrepreneurs struggle in defining a target market, thinking, "Well, I can sell to anybody!" This may be true; but do you really want just anybody? Instead, think about the clients you most enjoy working with, either because they are highly profitable or truly pleasurable to work with. Imagine most of your clients being exactly like this and then imagine what your business would be like. Would **you** be happier?

When describing to someone your target market, you want to detail exactly who you are looking to do business with, almost as if you were painting a picture of this group of people. Often, demographics and psychographics are used to help describe your target audience.

According to Webster's dictionary, these terms defined are:
Demographics: of or relating to the study of changes that occur in large groups of people over a period of time: of or relating to demography.
Psychographics: market research or statistics classifying population groups according to psychological variables (as attitudes, values, or fears); variables or trends identified through such research.

Demographics can further be broken down for **business-to-business** and **business-to-consumer** companies, and the list could go on, taking up several pages. Below are some of the top demographics used by entrepreneurs I work with.

Business-to-Business:

- Number of:
  o employees
  o locations
  o vehicles in fleet
  o phones
  o computers
- Type of ownership
- Geography (ZIP code, town/city, county, state)
- Service Area
- Retail/Wholesale/Online
- Office Space: Retail, Office, Warehouse, House

Business-to-Consumer:

- Occupation
- Age
- Gender
- Geography (ZIP code, town/city, county, state)
- Type of Dwelling
- Marital Status
- Kids
- Grandchildren
- Pets
- Hobbies
- Income
- Religion
- Political Affiliation
- Sexual Preference
- Type of Car
- Number of Vehicles
- Toys (RVs, ATV, Boat, Jet ski)
- Number of Properties Owned (home, rental, vacation)

Demographics help people see more precisely targets you are describing; as you are sharing your target market, be sure to be objective.

eTIFFANIE: When describing your target market, be objective, not subjective.

Why is being objective so important? Because being objective is based on distinct facts, rather than subjective, general feelings.

I often speak at Chambers of Commerce events, helping the members maximize their relationships as well as generate more referrals. Several years back at a Chamber of Commerce program, I asked a personal trainer to describe her target market and she replied, "Mature women". There are many directions we can go with that one, so I simply asked what her definition of a mature woman was, and she shared, "women over the age of 18". That answer was not what I had been expecting. When describing your target market, you want to portray in objective details.

The most common subjective descriptors I hear, and would like to eliminate, are:

- Small, Medium or Large Business
- Young or Old
- Lower, Middle, Upper Class
- Small or Large (perhaps denoting a house, though I have heard someone seeking overweight clients ask for "large people")

Instead of saying a "small business," paint the picture of what you intend: a company with less than 5, 50, 500 employees; a mom-and-pop shop; a single retail hub with a cash register near the door? The Small Business Administration defines a small business by its number of employees and revenue, and employees range from 50 employees to 1,500, hardly making for a clear, objective picture. The more **specific** you can be about what you are looking for, the more **terrific** the results will be!

(As my mentor, Tom Fleming, loves to share, "Be specific to be terrific.")

Once armed with demographics, further pinpoint your ideal client by using psychographics. Psychographics help classify clients' feelings toward the goods and services they purchase, which ideas and items they value, how they make purchasing decisions, and the factors that influence their lifestyles.

Examples of psychographics include:

- Social Class (by occupation, socio-economic position, etc.)
- Lifestyle (cataloging based on values, beliefs, opinions, or interests)
- Professional Status
- Values
- Loyalty
- Personality Characteristics

Applying demographics and psychographics - what is your target market? As you write down your thoughts, move from the "biggest" details to the finer points.

Here is an example:
Those in my target market own a condo and drive an SVU, are a member of a gym and have manicured nails, have never been married, and are women between the ages of 30 and 45.

Have a clear picture of this person? Perhaps not, so let's rearrange the details. Those in my target market are women, 30-45, never married, living in a condo and

4 ½ Networking Mistakes | **89**

driving a SVU. They are members of a local gym and have manicured nails.

The information is the same, simply structured differently to form a more precise, objective picture in the mind about your target market. You want to paint your target market starting with the bigger descriptors and funneling down. Notice how much easier it was to imagine a target when the description starts with women between the ages of 30 and 45 rather than ending with them.

Now, let's look at **your** target market. Take a minute to write it out.

Are you getting a clearer picture of what your target market looks like? Now work through a few questions to see if you can tighten it up.

Are there any subjective terms in your description? Take a peek at subjective terms, and then try to change them to objective ones. Go ahead, I will wait.

Are there any redundancies?
For example, with "70- to 100-year-old elderly couples," that could be narrowed to "couples 70+ years old."

eTIFFANIE: When marketing, *KISS*; Keep It Short and Simple.

Next, can you combine any of the descriptors? For example, instead of sharing, "I am looking to work with married couples. These couples have at least two children. Those children are under the age of 5." Simply say, "I am looking to work with married couples with at least two kids under the age of 5."

Now that you have your target market, I challenge you to share that target market with a couple of people to see if they can clearly picture it.

eTIFFANIE: Describe your target market so clearly that others quickly form a picture of the client as you have in mind.

Now that you have a firmer idea of your target market, look at **who** should be in your contact sphere. Remember, contact sphere relationships are with professionals who sell to your target market and are not in competition with you.

One of my favorite examples of a contact sphere comes from Dr. Ivan Misner, the father of modern networking, according to CNN. Dr. Misner's example is the "wedding mafia" who targets brides. It can include: event planners, caterers, venue owners, jewelers, florists, dressmakers, DJs, photographers, videographers, cake makers, and so on. All these people have the client, a bride, in common.

Look again at your target market and ask who is selling to that group of people besides you?

If you are having a hard time coming up with those professions selling to the group, it is likely:

- You don't know enough about them.
  eTIFFANIE: If you are wondering who is selling to people in your target market (potential contact sphere relationships), ask them!

- Your target market is still too broad and no specific seller is jumping out at you.

Be creative when thinking about contact sphere relationships, and remember that everyone wants referrals from bankers, financial advisors, realtors and CPAs. However, a lot fewer people ask funeral planners, golf pros, and car salesmen to be part of their referral team. Worth considering?

eTIFFANIE: Be creative and think outside of the box when coming up with contact sphere relationships. Know who is selling SPECIFICALLY to your target market.

Now that you know which professions should be in your contact sphere, take a look at your network. Do you already have people who deal with your ideal clients every day, or do you need to get out and find them? Remember, these are the people most likely to pass you **business all day, every day**!

Bonus Material: Creating your Funneling Conversation

I first learned about the funneling conversation from Tom Fleming when attending the Certified Networker® Program offered by the Referral Institute®. This powerful way to network is both a time saver and efficiency maker, allowing you to effectively determine if someone is part of your contact sphere or a prospect.

The funneling conversation arrives at that answer in a way that creates curiosity, stimulating instead of ending a conversation. Throughout this section, you will have the opportunity to create your own funneling conversation.

Here's a sample funneling conversation:

Sue and Tim are networking, and after engaging in small talk for a moment, Sue begins the funneling conversation.

Sue: *Tim, so tell me, what do you do?*

Tim: I am an underwater basket weaver.

Sue: *Interesting.*

Tim: What do you do, Sue?

Sue: *I help people relax.*

Tim: Wow. How do you do that?

Sue: *I have a few different techniques and products that I use to help people relax. Question, do you like to relax?*

Tim: I do.

Sue: *Are you interested in being able to relax more often?*

Tim: I would really like to relax more often.

Sue: *I work with people using massage to help people relax more often. Would you like to get together for a cup of tea and we can explore the various ways I might*

be able to help you relax more?
Tim: That would be great!

Tim and Sue set up the meeting before they leave the conversation.

There are several hidden elements within the conversation, which we will explore in this section. Do note that while the conversation flows easily, the goal of the funneling conversation is highly specific — to create results.

Parts of the funneling conversation

Step 1: "What do you do?"
When talking with someone you just met, it is natural to inquire about his/her profession, and 99 percent of the people you talk to while networking will respond with just that. Once you have the profession, you should first determine if the person it belongs to is a potential contact sphere relationship.

If the person fits that description (i.e., is in a non-competing profession that deals with your target market), share, "That's great! I find that in my business I have the opportunity to pass a lot of referrals to _____ (insert the profession here). Would you be open to getting together for coffee (or lunch, etc.) so we could get to know each other better and perhaps be able to pass along referrals over time?" The goal is to schedule a time to learn more about each other's business outside the event to potentially create a referral relationship.

If the person's profession is outside your contact sphere then you want to move on to the next part of the funnel. After learning the other's profession, **wait**. Compel that person to ask you in return, "What do you do?" If you are not asked, accept that the person probably is not interested in learning more about you, and move on, politely.

Step 2: "I help ..."
When you are asked, you want to respond with an answer based on how you benefit your clients, your "I help" statement, not with a textbook definition of your profession or an elevator pitch, but an answer based on how you benefit your clients. The value of this statement is in clearly answering why a client might seek out your product or service, without necessarily defining you by your profession. Avoiding such a stark definition is important, as the goal is to create curiosity for now.

By answering this way, you squarely shift the focus to the benefits you create for a client, rather than your profession's possibly mundane features. If intrigued, the person inquires after details — in most situations, asking "how?" — which is your permission to share more about your business. Again, if you are not asked, the person you are speaking to is not interested. Move on or leave the conversation.

Step 3: Prospecting
Once "How?" — or, "How do you do that?" — is raised you want to begin asking a series of questions that determine if the person is a prospect or not. Start with a qualifying question that can be answered easily with a simple "yes," (still a prospect) or "no," (not a prospect). Remember, if at any point in the funneling conversation

you get a "no," the conversation is over. You have identified someone is neither a prospect nor contact sphere. Move on.

If you continue receiving "yes," keep asking questions that qualify the person as a prospect, sharing through questions in this part of the funnel about the benefits of what you do.

Step 4: Ask
Should all questions elicit a "yes," great! The final part of the funneling conversation is to invite that person to take the next step in moving toward becoming a client.

Funneling Conversation Dos & Don'ts:
Do:

- Ask **yes or no** questions, remembering that "yes" answers mean still a prospect and "no" answers mean not a prospect. A "no" kicks people out of the funnel.

- Have two to four benefit-based questions to determine if the person you are conversing with could be a good prospect for you.

- Avoid open-ended questions that may or may not help give you the information you need or use them only as conversation starters. Concentrate on closed, yes/no questions.

- Funnel down. Start with a broad question and then move to more specific questions as you qualify the prospect. You do not want to schedule a post-event appointment or follow-up with someone unless that person is a prospect or referral source.

Don't:

- Include your profession, product or service in the "I help" statement.

- Ask open questions.

- Ask deep or very personal questions early. Start broad and then funnel your way down.

- Ask unrelated questions. The conversation should flow from one question to the next.

- Forget the next step, the call to action, at the end of your funneling conversation.

Preparing your Funneling Conversation:

Step 1: Think of those industries that deal with your target market most frequently, so you can more easily decide when networking if someone could be a potential contact sphere relationship. Write a handful or so of them in the spaces below.

Asking "What do you do?" means asking, "Are you the professional I am hoping to meet?"

-

-

-

-

-

-

Step 2: When asked what you do for work, how will you respond?

Think in a broad but enticing stroke how your products or services benefit your clients. "I help":

- people have fun

- entrepreneurs save time

- people feel confident

- create peace of mind

- people relax

- inspire happiness

- people make more money

- reduce people's stress

Creating your "I help" statement may be uncomfortable. However, by focusing **solely** on the **benefits** offered to your clients, you inspire people to want to know the "How" of what you do. If you lead with details of your profession, you choke off further questions, as people are inclined to lump you with others they know that do what you do.

Create a concise sentence summarizing what you do, without giving away too many details.

"I help

"

Step 3: Now you are ready to move through the prospect-qualifying part of the funneling conversation.

Create a series of two to four questions determining if the person would want to be a client of yours. These questions should communicate the **benefit** of choosing you and your company and be worded as closed questions, triggering "yes" or "no" answers only (i.e., no open-ended questions). Again, "yes" answers continue the process, a "no" means the person is not a prospect and kicks him or her out of the funnel.

This can be a challenging exercise. Take a few minutes to brainstorm qualifiers and disqualifiers for your business:

Qualifiers   Disqualifiers

Remember Sue and Tim's exchange? When asked, "How do you do that?" she replied: *I have a few different techniques and products that I use to help people relax.* **Do you like to relax?**

From your list above, what might be a good question to follow "how" for you?

Ask:

Double-check your question to see if you can answer yes to:

- Is your question focused on a benefit you offer?
- Can it easily be answered with a "yes" or "no"?
- If you receive a yes, is the person still a prospect?
- If you receive a no, is he/she no longer a prospect?
- Is it easy to ask a follow-up question?

Now create one to three more questions to further qualify the prospect.

Ask:

Ask:

Ask:

Step 4: By continuing to answer "yes" the person is primed to answer the next question affirmatively, as well. This is where you offer the appointment.

Start with a sentence briefly stating what you do to achieve the benefit(s) mentioned in the previous questions, and then ask to meet. Sue shared: *I work with people using massage to help people relax more often.*

Would you like to get together for a cup of tea and we can explore the various ways I might be able to help you relax more?

Now is the time to close the conversation and make an offer that moves you to the next step.
Your options could include:

- Book an appointment at your office (whether complimentary or paid)
- Meet for a beverage or meal
- Schedule a sales session or free consultation
- Sign up for a newsletter
- Attend an event or workshop you are hosting
- Follow up with _____ (be creative!)

What will be the next step you offer?

"Would you like to

If met with a "yes" your last question carries you to the next step, and you now know you have a qualified prospect!

By keeping **focused** when networking and using the funneling conversation you will be able to determine easily if the person you are speaking with is a potential contact sphere relationship, a prospect, or neither.

Recap:

Now we will revisit the earlier conversation with Sue and Tim, examining some of those hidden elements (highlighted **bold** asides):

Sue: *Tim, so tell me, what do you do?*
Tim: I am an underwater basket weaver.
Sue: *Interesting.*
Note that Sue responds to his profession, which she determines is not part of her contact sphere. She then waits for him to ask her the question in return. Had he been in her contact sphere she would have asked for the meeting.
Tim: What do you do, Sue?
Sue: *I help people relax.*
Here Sue shares her "I help" statement then waits for him to ask the follow-up question.
Tim: Wow. How do you do that?
Sue: *I have a few different techniques and products that I use to help people relax. Do you like to relax?*
Sue shared a simple sentence giving the details of what she does, and then asks her first qualifying question.
Tim: I do.
If Sue had received a "no" here, she would end the funneling conversation.
Sue: *Are you interested in being able to relax more often?*
Tim: I would really like to relax more often.
Sue: *I work with people using massage to help people relax more often. Would you like to get together for a cup of tea and we can explore the various ways I might be able to help you relax more?*
As Sue received "yes" answers, she shares what she does and follows through by asking for an

appointment.

Tim: That would be great!

Finally, Tim and Sue set up the meeting before they leave the event.

Now that you have all the details on the funneling conversation, write out your funneling conversation.

Funneling Conversation:

I help:

Ask:

Ask:

Ask:

Share:

Next Step:

Sample Funneling Conversations

Tiffanie Kellog of the Referral Institute®
(www.ReferralInstituteTampa.com)

- Ask: Are you looking to grow your business?

- Ask: Would referrals help you grow your business?

- Ask: Would you like to learn how to make $10,000 to $50,000 more in referrals this year?

- Share: What I do is work with entrepreneurs just like you to help them double, triple or even quadruple their referrals...

Next Step: If you would like to come to an upcoming program as my guest to learn more about growing your business by referral, please give me a business card and I will send you details for attending my next program.

Rob Kellog of Thread Art
(www.facebook.com/ThreadArtFL)
Client: Company participating in an upcoming expo or trade show

- Ask: Are you hoping to grow your business through the expo/trade show?

- Ask: Do you feel a strategy could help you create those results?

- Ask: Are you open to having a conversation to brainstorm a strategy to help you have a success tradeshow?

- Share: I work with companies just like yours to help them maximize their results.

Next Step: Would you be interested in getting together next week for a consultation?

Christopher Clarke of Therapeutic Elements Center for Massage Therapy (www.BookaMassageNow.com) Client: Athletes who train at a Crossfit gym in the Tampa Bay area

- Ask: Do you work out with a personal trainer?

- Ask: Do you feel sore after the workout?

- Ask: Would you be interested in alleviating some of the soreness and increasing your performance?

- Share: I like working with athletes just like you through massage therapy to help them maximize their efforts in training.

Next Step: Would you visit www.BookaMassageNow.com to read client testimonials and book an appointment online?

Advanced Funneling Conversations
Combining your Funneling Conversation with Behavioral Styles

As you become more comfortable with networking and the funneling conversation and familiar with the Room Full of Referrals® (*Bonus Material: Behavioral Styles*), think of creating a funneling conversation for each of the four styles.

- Go-Getters (D) - results
- Promoters (I) - fun
- Nurturers (S) - relationships
- Examiners (C) – effectiveness/efficiency

Or, can you create a single funneling conversation that hits on all styles?

Bonus Material: 8 Types of Referral Sources

from the Certified Networker® Program

There are many different people in your network and many of them are potential referral source, of which there are eight different kinds.

1. Clients:

Clients often are thought of as the best potential referral sources and they make **powerful** referral sources because they have used your product/service and know what an amazing job you do. Not all are referral sources, though; some will be content just to be clients and will not refer you.

Give some thought to how you could inspire your clients to pass you referrals. Concentrate on your **raving fans**, those people who are happy to help you with your business because they **love** your product/service.

2. Members of Networking Organizations

Members of your networking organization understand the value of a referral, and often work with a Giver's Gain® mentality, knowing if you give referrals to others you will, in turn, gain referrals. People you see consistently while networking can be great referral sources, especially if you are a member of a referral-generating group. One of the largest such networking organizations is BNI (www.bni.com); BNI is a one-per-profession organization that meets to help its members generate referrals.

Do note that some organizations concentrate heavily on referrals, while others take a different focus.

3. People Who Have Given You Referrals

People who already have given you referrals have acquired the "know, like, and trust" necessary to give you more referrals. Turn to them; they probably might do it again!

4. People You Have Given Referrals To

Relationships last only as long as they are beneficial to both parties. If you have been **giving** referrals to the relationship, it may be time for you to **receive** a referral. All that may be needed is for you to ask!

5. People Whose Business Benefits from Yours

Whenever you get a referral, does someone else in your network also benefit?

Think about your vendors and suppliers, or other people in your network. If someone else benefits from the referrals you receive, that person is a **powerful** source with a vested interest in your success. For example, every time a realtor gets a referral (at least here in Florida) then a title agent, home inspector, and mortgage company usually gets a referral as well.

6. Staff Members

Every single member of your staff has a vested interest in the success of your company, not just your sales staff. Keep them happy and arm them with what they need to pass additional referrals along to you. (For tips, read *Bonus Material: Arming your Staff to Pass You Referrals.*)

7. People with Whom You Do Business

Money is a powerful motivator, and anyone buying a product/service from someone has their complete attention.

Think about where you spend your money — a hair stylist, chiropractor, dry cleaner — and seize the opportunity. As a client of the business, ask the owner to support you in growing your business by passing referrals. Being a client gives you the opening to ask for a referral.

8. Contact Sphere Relationships

I saved the best for last. These are the people who are in a non-competing profession with the same clients as you.

Bonus Material: Arming your Staff to Pass Referrals

Are you missing out on easy referrals? You just might be!

Every single employee has a vested interest in your business being successful, as success bolsters the likelihood of their getting paid every week. In addition, the added value they bring to the organization makes for a more hopeful future for everyone.

A key consideration in this conversation is expanding your thinking so that **all** of your employees have the potential to pass you business, in addition to the sales staff. Encourage your entire staff, including your receptionist, "widget" makers and service people, your delivery staff, etc., to be on the lookout for new clients

Keep a few crucial points in mind when preparing your staff to be referral sources. First, you are going to need to educate employees regarding the relevant points of your business, including:

- who is an ideal client and who makes up your target market
- key phrases to listen for and, perhaps, clues to look for that indicate someone may need your product or service
- how to create the referral, and how to bring their business into the office

Another crucial training component will be to encouraging your staff to horn toot, by replying to "How are you doing?" with a response that shares positive going ons within the company.

The next step in creating these referral sources is arming them with the right collateral material. Collateral material gives your staff a sense of pride in what you do, a strong identity of their role within the team, and keeps your branding consistent.

Offer all employees personalized business cards, including:

- Employee's name and title

- Company's website and social media information

- The staff member's direct contact information, perhaps including a personalized email instead of "info@___.com"

- The basic product/services/benefits offered by your company, as your staff may not be as fluent in the language of your business

Last, and certainly not least, recognize and reward your staff for bringing you business!

Bonus Material: Creative Business Cards

Every entrepreneur has, or should have, business cards; very few give their cards the consideration they deserve.

My intention here is to explore some thoughts when it comes to business cards. Know that there is no right or wrong, no good or bad, when it comes to your card, just points I want to stress.

When networking, your business card is what you leave behind with the people you meet with the hope they will remember you. Essentially, it is an extension of you. I have to ask: Does your business card match who **you are** and what you represent?

eTIFFANIE: Your business cards, like all your marketing materials, should MATCH who you are and what you do!

As an entrepreneur (whether you own your own business, work on commission, or represent a franchise/MLM), **you are your brand**. You have a product or service to offer, but when it comes to referral-based marketing, **you are selling yourself**. Will your card help to make you more memorable, or will you — like your card — simply fade away?

Let's start with the basics... What are the musts for your business card?

• Your name

• Contact information

Yep. That is all that is required for a business card. Some of the most dramatic cards are void of multiple phone numbers and addresses, website and social media information, and whatever else might be piled on. As with your networking, more is not necessarily better. Think, what important pieces of identification are a **must** for your business card?

Other identifiers you may want on your business card — and please pick from these options, you will not want them all — include:

- Address (important if you have a retail location)
- Email
- Phone Number
- Fax Number (if you still rely on faxes; these are quickly going the way of pagers)
- Website
- Social Media (one or two links ideally, unless you are a social media consultant)
- Tag Line
- Mission Statement
- Products/Services offered
- License Number (a requirement for some industries)

Between the internet and social media, business cards no longer need to display every detail. Better to use your business card to direct prospective clients to your website, where you can display visually and in words the many products and services your business offers.

Now that we know **what** information we need on the business card, let's consider the design. I do encourage **all** my clients to do what I have done, and **hire a professional graphic designer**. Some printers will have a graphic designer in house, while others will not.

eTIFFANIE: Your business card is a CRUCIAL piece of your marketing material; hire a professional to help you design one that represents YOU!

Considerations include:

- Font
- Font size (if your market is senior citizens, you want an easy-to-read card)
- Color
- Single or double-sided (just because you have two sides does not mean you have to use them)
- Logo
- Headshot
  While a headshot is not a requirement, people do think in pictures. If they can see you when they think of you, they may even feel like they know you better, leading to more business for you, and sooner.

Once you have made these decisions and a professionally designed card is in hand, you have the opportunity to work with a printer. Business cards are a standard size, though ample options exist for the paper they are printed on. Do you want a strong, sturdy card, or the low-cost option? Remember, your business cards are an extension of you and your business, and make sure everything about them reflects this.

Before I began training and speaking with people about growing their business by referral, I spent a few years in marketing. My husband owns a promotional items company and there are a number **of non-traditional business cards** that can be used to set you apart from everyone else in networking. I interviewed my husband, Rob, to come up with this list from his top-selling business cards at www.threadartfl.com.

MATERIAL:

- Plastic and Metal. These business cards, whether made from plastic, aluminum or similar materials, are the same size and shape as traditional business cards, and can include much of the same information, but are limited to one or two colors.

- Business Card Magnets. These are one of Thread Art's top-selling items as well as the top business card alternative. The thicker material makes people less likely to throw the cards away, and they can easily be slapped onto a metal surface. A piece of advice... in addition to your information, add something memorable or useful to encourage people to keep it.

- Magnifying Glass. This card is a similar size/shape as the traditional business card, with an actual magnifying glass embedded, leaving only a small area for your information. If your target market is geared toward seniors, this card is a **perfect** card for you — and for them to keep it in their wallets and pull out when there is fine print to read.

- Eye Glass Cleaner: Perhaps we should simply call these cards cleaning cloths. With the boom in touch-screen electronics (smartphones, laptops, tablets) in addition to eyeglasses or sunglasses, this item is increasingly popular. Reasonably priced, it includes a large area for your information, and a full color and photographic imprint is available. There also are options for cases for the cloths, including one shaped like a business card.

- M&Ms® – Yep, you are reading that right! This is one of my favorites, as I love M&Ms®! These plastic containers hold a business card as well as a favorite chocolate treat. Want to take it one step further? Put your logo or photograph on your M&Ms®.

- Mint Business Cards: Again, similar in size and shape to the traditional business card, just a tad thicker due to the mint in the middle. **Great** when networking if the person really needs a mint, unless they realize you are sharing **because** they need a mint. The similar-size, multipurpose Hand Sanitizers business cards may be a perfect follow-up to a mint, too.

- Playing Cards and Poker Chips: While two very different items, I lumped these together because they often are found together, at least when playing poker. The poker chips are compact and memorable, but have a limited printing area. One tip, if you can put a local team (professional or college, taking care if your area is full of rivals) or cause (think pink ribbon) on one side and your logo on the other, you may increase the staying power.
  The playing cards, similar in size to business cards, give plenty of space for your words, and, if it is your style, you can ask people when networking to "pick a card, any card."

As these options show, you can make your cards memorable ... and be the one professional who sticks out — in a good way — in the minds of the people you meet.

Don't stop at my ideas for creating a **powerful** business card. You also can Google business cards, read books on business cards (the first book I read on this was *It's in the Cards* by Dr. Ivan Misner, which gave me ideas for two wildly successful ones), and talk to marketing experts, etc.

Remember my eTIFFANIE when it comes to business cards:
eTIFFANIE: When networking, give out your business card ONLY when you are asked!

Bonus Material: Behavioral Style

By Dawn Lyons, Partner with the Referral Institute and BNI Executive Director in San Francisco Bay Area

Some of the best tips for networking begin with understanding who you are and what your strengths are. When we realize what it is that we bring to each conversation, we can see how to adapt in that conversation to make it an incredible experience for all involved. At the Referral Institute®, we have identified four major behavioral styles (based on the DiSC® profile). Let's share them with you so you can understand who you truly are.

Go-Getters

Definition: A hustling, enterprising type of person. The Go-Getter would be the equivalent of the "D" in the DiSC® language.

Go-Getters tend to be very results-oriented, driven, fast-paced and in many cases impatient. They have a "get it done now" attitude. They attend networking events to gain new business and look to meet the most successful people at the event. They tend to be very challenge-oriented and speak with very few words because they can be more productive with fewer words. They are not afraid to bend the rules. They figure it is easier to beg forgiveness than to ask permission. They are so focused that they can even appear aloof or unapproachable.

While networking, Go-Getters will tend to manage the conversation. They seek to understand what might be "attractive" about continuing the conversation with you and as long as you are competent, succinct, and intriguing, they are in!

If you would like a conversation that makes you attractive to them, include some of these questions emphasizing how you can help them, and then **do it**!

- What are the best clients for you?
- Which professions refer you most often?
- What are three business goals I might be able to help you with?

As you can see, these are very specific and geared to the Go-Getter's benefit. Here is the thing, if you give them some type of result quickly, they will find you "attractive." Receiving results are very important to them. The key here is that once you have shown a Go-Getter results, they are much more committed to doing something for you. See, they also have a strong desire to win; so, in the language of giving referrals, they will want to give more to you whenever possible.

Promoters

Definition: An active supporter, someone who urges the adoption of, or attempts to sell or popularize someone or something. The Promoter would be the equivalent of the "I" in the DISC® language.

Promoters tend to be very positive, friendly, and "happy go lucky" people. They love to be on the go and are okay with having lots of irons in the fire. They avoid confrontation and seek fun in everything they do.

Promoters can be easily distracted and would rather go to lunch with clients or referral sources than work on a deadline in the office. They tend to utilize their enthusiasm and excitement to influence others. They are risk-takers who are not inclined to do their homework or check out information, and base many of their decisions on intuition.

While networking, Promoters like to hang out, meet new people, talk to their friends and make sure they are "seen" at the event. They enjoy connecting people and even being the life of the party.

Ask these types of questions to be seen as someone they will enjoy talking to and, ultimately, building a deeper relationship with.

- What do you love about what you do?
- What do you do for fun when you aren't working?
- Do you have favorite clients... if so, what do they look like?
- Who would you love to meet while you are here networking?

These types of questions will keep the conversation upbeat, fun, and enjoyable for them, which in turn will have them wanting to spend more time with you.

Nurturers

Definition: Someone who gives tender care and protection to a person or thing, especially to help it grow or develop. The Nurturer would be the equivalent to the "S" in the DiSC® language.

Nurturers tend to be very patient, kind, caring, and helpful people. They are great listeners and tend to enjoy things at a slower pace than the Go-Getters and Promoters. They do not liked to be pushed or rushed, and appreciate quality time with people. They attend networking functions to connect with people they already know, meet a few down-to-earth people and focus on deepening their relationships.

Nurturers have relaxed dispositions, which make them approachable and warm. They develop strong networks of people who are willing to be mutually supportive and reliable. They are excellent team players due to their supportive attitude.

You can ask these types of questions to begin developing a strong relationship with them.

- How long have you lived in the area?

- Where is your family located?

- What got you started in your business?

- Tell me what you enjoy most about your business?

- What type of clients do you enjoy working with the most?

- What is the long-term benefit of clients working with you?

As you can see, these types of questions evoke even more conversation, allowing you to go deeper into who they are and what they really enjoy. Do spend enough time with them so they feel like they got to know you. They are more concerned about who you are than what it is you do.

Examiners

Definition: A person who inspects or analyzes a person, place or thing in detail, while testing their knowledge or skill by asking questions. The Examiner would be the equivalent of the "C" in the DiSC® language.

Examiners tend to be very thorough, efficient, task-driven people. They seek information and knowledge, and love to check things off their "to do" list. Because Examiners need a lot of information, they tend to make decisions more slowly than the Go-Getters and Promoters. They have a propensity toward perfectionism.

While networking, Examiners tend to be very good conversationalists as they know a lot about a lot of topics. They attend networking functions only to market their business and, once they achieve their goal for the evening, they usually leave as quickly as they can. Whenever possible they like to have a job to do at the function, helping with registration, timekeeping, etc. This allows them to have something to do while they network and is much more comfortable for them.

You can ask them these types of questions to learn more about them:

- What do you do?

- How long have you been doing it?

- What is your specialty?

- Which types of clients do you prefer to work with?

- Are there strategic professions that often refer you?

Hopefully, by now you can see a bit of a trend in the questions, and yet just changing a few things make the questions more pertinent to each of the styles. Knowing this while networking can prove to be incredibly valuable to you in order to ensure you make the best impression you can!

Try to decide which behavioral style you would say is your highest style. Yes, you are a blend of all four styles, but if you had to declare one, which would it be? Okay, now that you know that, please utilize the strengths that we mention for your style even more! Using your strengths first will make networking very enjoyable and valuable to you and your business. In order to challenge yourself, ask some of those questions that appeal to the other styles more often. As you do, you will get more comfortable with them, attain better results while networking, make a better first impression, and definitely deepen and strengthen relationships more quickly!

It's that easy. To be a better networker, know yourself and the strengths you bring to the table in every conversation, and know other people's behavioral style, and watch as a better experience unfolds for all involved!

For more information on this material, please read the Amazon.com best-seller "Room Full of Referrals...and How To Network For Them" by Dr. Tony Alessandra, Dr. Ivan Misner, and Dawn Lyons.

Bonus Material: The Power of the Handwritten Card
By Paula Bonnell, Owner of Aslite Enterprises (a gratitude and acknowledgement company specializing in cards) and BNI Managing Director in West Central Florida

One of the primary objectives of networking is to build relationships and one of the most effective and cost-effective ways of doing this is through the handwritten card. Here are a few facts about the greeting card industry in recent years:

- Americans purchase 6.5 billion greeting cards per year. (Annual retail of $7-$8 billion.)
  o The most popular card is a birthday card
  o The most popular seasonal card, by mail, is a Christmas card (1.6 billion units, including boxed sets)
  o The second most popular card, by mail, is a Valentine's Day card (145 million units)
- Social media is impacting card sending
- People under 30 sum up their ability to acknowledge and be acknowledged online, through social media, as such:
  o You and what's going on in your life is more broadly **known**, but you're less closely **connected**.

The difference between a physical card, online e-cards, and social media options is in the **impact** they make and the **connection** they create.

For example, how many of you saved your last e-card or "happy birthday" sentiment received social media? Very few, actually, as many e-cards have a "shelf life" so they are unable to be saved.

On the other hand, think about the physical cards you've received — a thank you, happy birthday, thinking of you or anniversary card. No doubt, you have some either displayed on your desk or carefully preserved in a box.

What determines whether you keep a card? The cards people discard are the impersonal, generic, untailored cards — the cards that say "thank you for your business" and nothing else. The cards people keep are those with some personal message that resonates with the receiver. And, this is true whether you're talking about cards sent to a customer or patient, or to a friend or family member.

The purpose of giving a card is so the receiver knows you value him or her, and thinks well enough of you to expend personal time. In a typical networking event, you could shake hands and exchange business cards with 20 to 100 people. How will you make yourself memorable to them? What moves your relationship from a handshake to a willingness to have coffee? The personal touch: the first impression you make and how well you connect in your follow-up contact.

There are three key components to creating a thank you card with impact:

1. Your intention in wanting to send a card to someone
2. That it is handwritten
3. What you're expressing shows authentic **gratitude.**

Intention is the 1st Key

If you're giving people cards because it's something you think you "should do," there will be little or no positive impact and, in fact, the response may be a little negative.

Your **intention** is **energy**.

Receiving a pre-printed thank you card with a signature you are unable to discern has made no impact. The person mailing the card has communicated to you that you are a business card in a pile of business cards, you made no particular impression on the sender, and the two of you have little or no connection. These cards typically get discarded without follow-up.

If, however, there is a note in your card highlighting something you said, something you both found in common, or some shared experience during that networking event, then a completely different type of communication is in play. The sender went through the effort of personalizing the note to make sure that you know you made an impression and a connection — at least for the sender. That is an attention-getter, has a more powerful, positive impact, and begins to build a relationship.

Maximize the impact of the card you're sending with this second key component.

Handwritten is the 2nd Key

Creating a connection by personalizing the card you mail is a great first step. If you want to enhance the impact, handwrite what you wish to express.

Your intention is energy. The words you choose have energy. The physicality of pen to paper is energy. All of that translates into a more impactful experience for the card's receiver.

Now, let me just say this — there are online resources available for a typewritten sentiment and companies that will address, stamp and mail the card. Sending out something with a personal touch is of benefit. If you have a database of 500 people, writing a note to each could be difficult and time-consuming. But to **maximize your impact** on the receiver, the card needs to be handwritten.

Gratitude is the 3rd Key

How do you know if you connect with someone? Typically, some kind of is emotion present, because emotion is what moves people to action. You can always create a card that reads, Thank You – It was great to meet you. But, if you're not clear about why you were grateful, specifically, you won't maximize your impact.

Here are some rules of thumb when writing cards to begin building business relationships:

1. Have **one** intention when you create a card — to create a connection. Please avoid asking for a sale or referrals in the guise of a thank you card. People immediately dismiss you and your card.
2. Be genuine with your sentiments. People easily sense false gratitude or attempted manipulation.
3. Spend your time wisely; mail cards to only those people with whom you feel a connection.
4. Do use handwritten cards as a networking tool.

Bonus Material: Taking Networking Online

By Courtney Nestler, owner of Bright Light Solutions (a social media training & marketing company)

We all meet potential clients and referral partners at networking functions and events. But what do you do with those stacks of cards with random notes on the back? One good option is to add them to your online follow-up system, connecting through social media, signing up on their website for their newsletter, or asking permission to add them to your email list. In this chapter, we are going to focus on social media as a tool.

Get Connected

Whether it's one or several days after the event, take time to do a little research. If prospective clients or referral sources have a website, which is more than likely, their social media platforms will be easily accessible. If not, no worries — run a search for them on multiple platforms. Depending on their industry and target market, they could be on a few to multiple platforms. Start with the more popular first and work your way down. Begin by following their professional pages and accounts, as not everyone is open to connecting immediately on a personal level. Usually, enough information is available for you to determine if you have any connection points or common interests.

Motivating Your Network

Once you are connected with these people, using social media is a great way to motivate them to take action on your behalf. One easy way to help these potential clients and referral partners is to share their information through the social media channels. This could be sharing their entire page, sharing a special they are having, sharing information on an event, or the like. As they take notice, they will want to help you in return. Another way to motivate your network is to leave reviews and recommendations. Of course, you'll want to take time to get to know them better and understand their business before you do this, but understand the importance. The stronger your relationship, the better your chance of them reaching out to connect with you online personally. Once you are connected, you can follow the goings on in their lives, good or bad, and you use them as triggers to reach out. And you'll know better what types of information, articles, and links capture their interest.

Be Aware

Social media also can work against you and actually hurt your chances of success in business. Most people don't think through the impact personal actions can have on business outcomes. So, before you start connecting with others on a personal level through social media, take a moment to re-evaluate your accounts. Go back through your photos, your 'About Me' section, your posts, and make sure there isn't anything overtly damaging to your chances for future business. Yes, it is your personal account, but people do business with those who they know, like and trust, and the untoward could wreak havoc on your reputation. Once you have your accounts clean, ask yourself a few questions before posting for the world to see.

1. Will This Hurt Anyone?
Is what you are about to post going to hurt anyone in any way? Sometimes we get upset or angry with life. That is normal. But blasting it out to the world is not always

appropriate. And using ALL CAPS won't make it any better.

2. Is This Too Much Information?

This is a broad umbrella question, covering the deeply personal facts/issues of the moment to posting about your ham and cheese sandwich. They're just too much. So, too, are scantily clad photos of you on vacation or the 100th picture of your cat. No one wants to know or cares to know this much information about you.

3. Will I Regret This Later?

This can go in many different directions as well. It could be a buzzed post from happy-hour at your local watering hole, to a long rant about your boss. There could be legal issues involved if you're in a car accident while posting, make slanderous online comments, or post other foolishness, like action shots in the midst of a workers' compensation claim. Take the time to think about whether you may regret that text or photo.

4. Would I Say This in Real Life?

Odds are, if you wouldn't say certain things to actual people, you probably shouldn't be posting them either. That is what journals are for in the privacy of your home. What's in your post is blasted for the entire world to see, forever.

5. Why Am I Posting This?

What is your motive or goal with a particular post? Are you gloating about how awesome you are? Are you bemoaning a horrible day and want everyone to know? Think about exactly why you are sharing information with the world. It's not just your friends who will be seeing your posts or photos. It could be a potential client, referral partner, a co-worker, too.

Keep these questions in mind before posting on either personal or business accounts now and spare yourself damage control in the future. Also, if you are going to use social media for business it's best to be an active user. One of the worst things you can do is set up a profile or page and never look at it again. Social media is interactive. It is in real time. By ignoring it, it won't go away. Depending on the generation, those you are targeting may rely heavily on it for their communications. Stay active so you can respond to direct messages, mentions, posts and tags, portraying yourself as a professional with a positive online reputation, and positioning yourself as a resource for others.